ZURICH

TRAVEL GUIDE 2025-2026

Hike Uetliberg, Cruise Lake Zurich, Explore Old Town, Climb Grossmünster, and Stroll Bahnhofstrasse – With Maps, Detailed Itineraries and Full-Color Photos

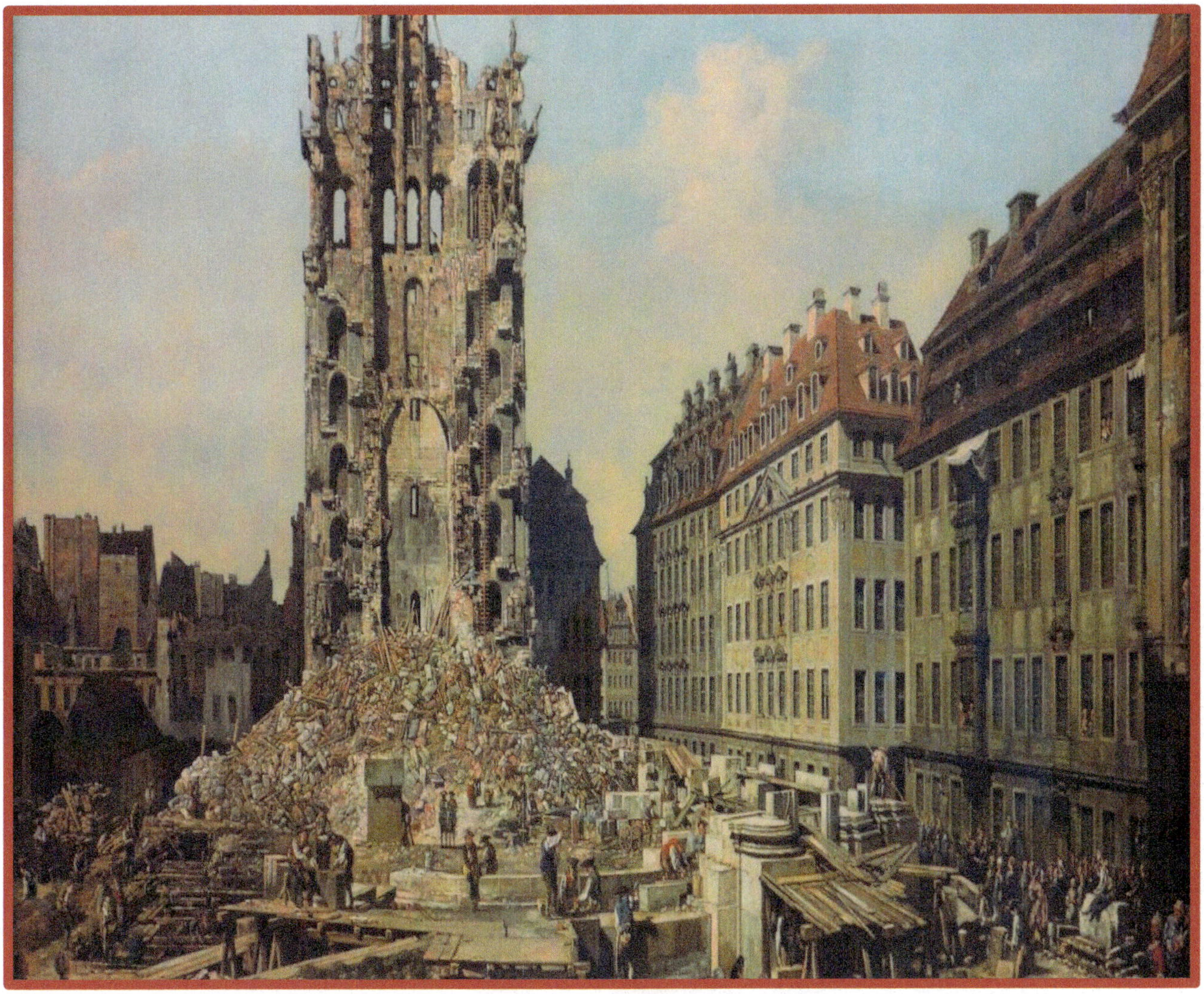

Dominic R. Fairmont

COPYRIGHT

TABLE OF CONTENTS

Chapter 1. Introduction to Zurich

Zurich is Switzerland's largest city and one of Europe's most vibrant cultural and financial hubs. Known for its picturesque setting on Lake Zurich, nestled against the backdrop of the Swiss Alps, the city seamlessly blends its rich history with modern innovation. Whether you're drawn to Zurich for its historic Old Town, world-class museums, culinary delights, or access to outdoor adventures, this guide will help you uncover the city's charm and maximize your experience.

1.1 Why Visit Zurich in 2025?

Zurich offers an exceptional mix of historical, cultural, and modern attractions, making it a must-visit destination in 2025. Here's why this year is an ideal time to explore the city:

1. The Renaissance of Travel and Tourism

After a challenging few years for global travel, Zurich is celebrating a revival of tourism in 2025. With newly renovated attractions, enhanced public transport systems, and an emphasis on sustainable travel, the city is more accessible and welcoming than ever.

2. Major Events and Festivals

- Zurich Film Festival (September–October): One of Europe's premier film festivals, showcasing global talent and featuring exclusive screenings.
- Street Parade (August): The world's largest techno parade returns, filling Zurich's streets with music, dance, and joy.

- Sechseläuten (April): This traditional spring festival, complete with the ceremonial burning of the "Böögg" (a snowman effigy), offers a glimpse into Zurich's cultural heritage.
- Art Basel in Zurich: An exclusive extension of the world-renowned art fair is expected to host exciting exhibitions and installations.

3. Culinary and Wine Scene

Zurich is becoming a hotspot for food lovers, with an increasing number of Michelin-starred restaurants, farm-to-table initiatives, and innovative Swiss cuisine. In 2025, new dining concepts, including floating restaurants on Lake Zurich, are making waves.

4. Nature Meets Urban Sophistication

Zurich's unique appeal lies in its proximity to nature. In just minutes, you can transition from the city center to hiking trails on Mount Uetliberg or enjoy boating on Lake Zurich. The city's emphasis on preserving green spaces ensures a harmonious balance between urban and natural environments.

5. Sustainable Travel Initiatives

Zurich is at the forefront of sustainable travel. From eco-friendly hotels to green energy-powered public transport, the city offers guilt-free exploration for environmentally conscious travelers. In 2025, Zurich continues its commitment to becoming one of the world's greenest cities.

6. Architectural and Historical Marvels

The city's architecture tells a story of its evolution. Explore medieval lanes in the Old Town (Altstadt), marvel at modern skyscrapers in Zurich West, and visit landmarks like the Grossmünster and Fraumünster churches, which have been enhanced with immersive experiences in 2025.

7. Gateway to Switzerland and Beyond

Zurich is the perfect base for exploring Switzerland. With its efficient train network, you can easily take day trips to iconic destinations like Lucerne, Interlaken, and Zermatt. Zurich Airport also serves as a global hub, making the city an ideal starting point for European adventures.

8. 2025 Travel Perks and Deals

To attract more visitors, Zurich tourism boards are offering exclusive discounts on the Zurich Card in 2025, which provides unlimited public transport, free entry to museums, and discounts on various tours and activities.

Zurich in 2025 is a city that celebrates its traditions while embracing innovation and sustainability. Whether you're a history enthusiast, art lover, outdoor adventurer, or food connoisseur, Zurich promises an unforgettable experience.

1.2 A Brief History of Zurich

Zurich's rich history stretches back more than 2,000 years, making it one of Europe's most historically significant cities. From its early days as a Roman settlement to its rise as a financial powerhouse, Zurich has continuously evolved while preserving its cultural heritage.

Early Beginnings: Celtic and Roman Roots

- The area now known as Zurich was first inhabited by the Celts around 500 BCE.
- In 15 BCE, the Romans established a military post called *Turicum* along the Limmat River. This settlement grew into a key trading hub due to its strategic location connecting northern and southern Europe.
- Roman ruins, including a customs post and baths, can still be seen in Zurich, offering a glimpse into its ancient past.

Medieval Growth and Prosperity

- By the 9th century, Zurich had become an important religious and political center, thanks to the founding of the Fraumünster Abbey in 853 by King Louis the German. The abbey played a significant role in the city's governance, especially under the rule of powerful abbesses.
- During the Middle Ages, Zurich grew into a prosperous trading town, known for its textiles and crafts. Its fortified walls and prime location made it a key player in regional politics.

Joining the Swiss Confederation

- In 1351, Zurich joined the Swiss Confederation, becoming one of its most influential members. This alliance helped the city secure its independence from external powers and foster its economic and cultural development.
- The Grossmünster Church became a focal point of the Protestant Reformation in the 16th century, led by Huldrych Zwingli, one of the movement's major figures. His influence shaped Zurich into a hub of religious and intellectual reform.

Industrial Revolution and Economic Powerhouse

- The 19th century saw Zurich's transformation into an industrial and financial center. The construction of railways connected the city to the rest of Europe, boosting trade and commerce.
- Zurich emerged as the banking capital of Switzerland, with institutions like Credit Suisse and UBS establishing their roots here.

20th Century: Modernization and Neutrality

- During both World Wars, Switzerland maintained its neutrality, and Zurich benefited as a center of diplomacy and intellectual exchange. It became a haven for artists, writers, and political exiles.
- The Dada art movement was founded in Zurich in 1916 at the Cabaret Voltaire, showcasing the city's avant-garde cultural influence.

Today: A Blend of Tradition and Innovation

- In the 21st century, Zurich is celebrated as a global financial hub, cultural hotspot, and sustainability leader. Its blend of medieval charm and modern architecture creates a unique urban experience.
- Despite its cosmopolitan nature, Zurich retains its small-town feel, with vibrant neighborhoods, historic landmarks, and a deep connection to Swiss traditions.

Zurich's history is one of resilience, innovation, and cultural richness. Each era has left its mark, creating a city that offers visitors a fascinating journey through time.

1.3 Zurich at a Glance: Key Facts and Highlights

Zurich is a city of contrasts, seamlessly blending its rich historical heritage with modern innovation and cosmopolitan flair. Here's a snapshot of Zurich's key features to help you get acquainted with the city:

Key Facts About Zurich

- **Location**:
  Zurich is located in north-central Switzerland, situated along the shores of Lake Zurich and the Limmat River, with the Swiss Alps visible in the distance.

- **Population**:
  Approximately 440,000 residents in the city proper, making it the largest city in Switzerland, with over 1.5 million people in the metropolitan area.

- **Official   Language:**
  Swiss German (*Züritüütsch*) is the main spoken dialect, but standard German is widely used. English is commonly spoken in tourist areas and business settings.

- **Currency:**
  Swiss Franc (CHF), though Euros are sometimes accepted in larger establishments.

- **Time   Zone:**
  Central European Time (CET), UTC +1. Daylight Saving Time applies from late March   to   late   October.

- **Climate:**
  Zurich experiences a temperate climate with distinct seasons:

  - Spring (March-May): Mild and blossoming.
  - Summer (June-August): Warm, perfect for outdoor activities.
  - Autumn (September-November): Cool with vibrant foliage.
  - Winter (December-February): Cold with occasional snow, ideal for nearby skiing.

Highlights of Zurich

- **Cultural   Capital   of   Switzerland:**
  With over 50 museums, 100 art galleries, and a world-renowned opera house, Zurich offers a wealth of cultural experiences. Highlights include the Kunsthaus Zurich   (art   museum)   and   the   Swiss   National   Museum.

- **Old   Town   (Altstadt):**
  Wander through the cobblestone streets of the Altstadt, home to medieval buildings, charming squares, and iconic landmarks like the Grossmünster and Fraumünster   churches.

- **Lake   Zurich   and   the   Limmat   River:**
  Perfect for scenic boat rides, waterfront dining, and leisurely strolls. The lake's crystal-clear waters and stunning views of the Alps make it a centerpiece of the city.

- **Bahnhofstrasse:**
  One of the world's most exclusive shopping streets, offering a mix of luxury boutiques,   Swiss   watchmakers,   and   department   stores.

- **Zurich West:**
  A former industrial district transformed into a trendy area known for its modern architecture, street art, and vibrant nightlife.

- **World-Class Cuisine:**
  Zurich is a culinary paradise, offering everything from traditional Swiss fondue and raclette to Michelin-starred dining experiences. Don't miss trying local specialties like *Zürcher Geschnetzeltes* and Swiss chocolates.

- **Outdoor Activities:**
  Enjoy hiking and cycling trails in and around the city, or head to Mount Uetliberg for panoramic views of Zurich and beyond.

- **Events and Festivals:**
  Zurich hosts a range of events throughout the year, including the Street Parade, Zurich Film Festival, and the traditional Sechseläuten festival.

- **Gateway to Switzerland:**
  Zurich serves as a convenient starting point for exploring Switzerland's iconic destinations, including the Swiss Alps, Rhine Falls, and charming towns like Lucerne.

Map © ontheworldmap.com - Source:
https://ontheworldmap.com/switzerland/map-of-switzerland-hd.jpg

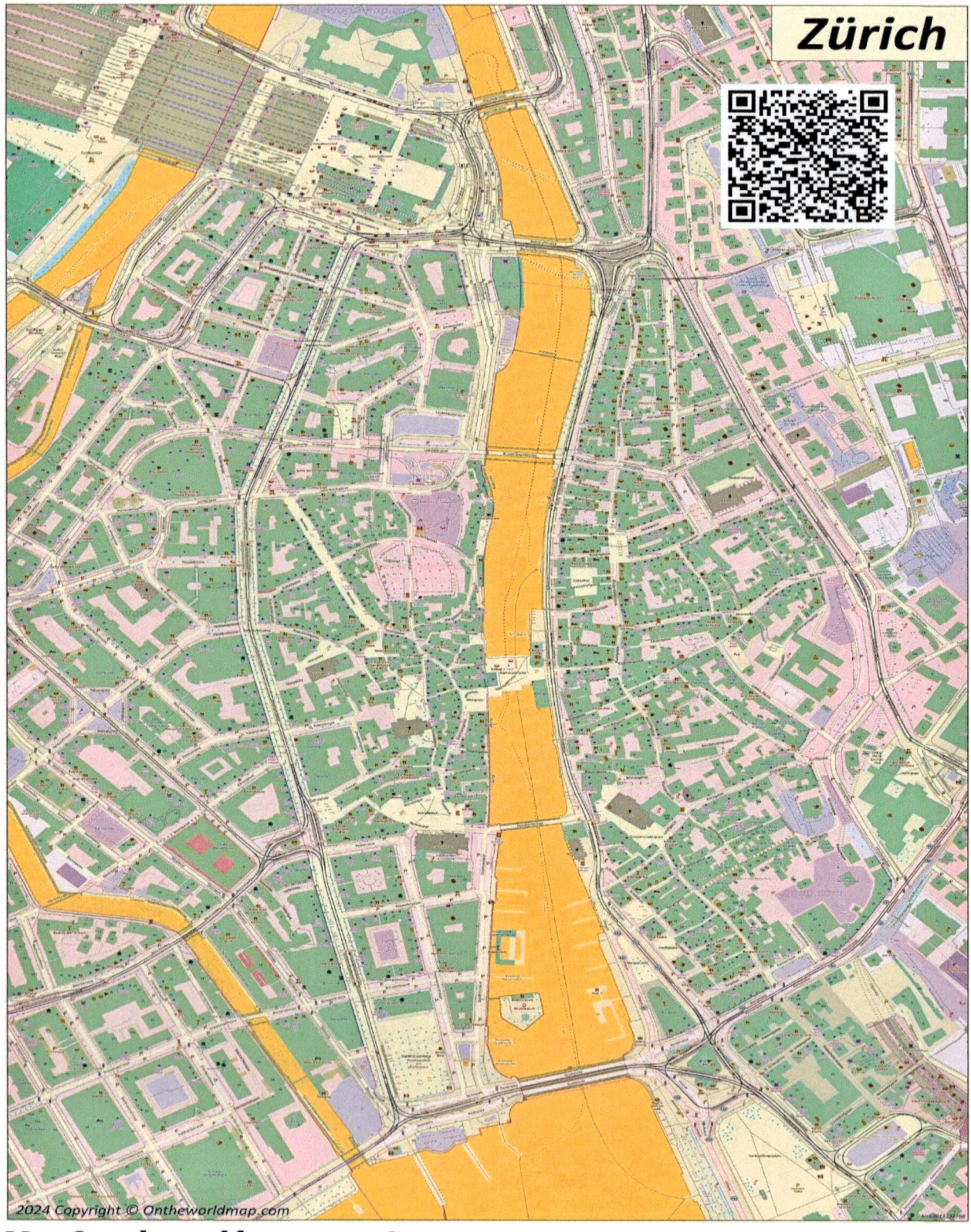

Map © ontheworldmap.com - Source:

Zürich

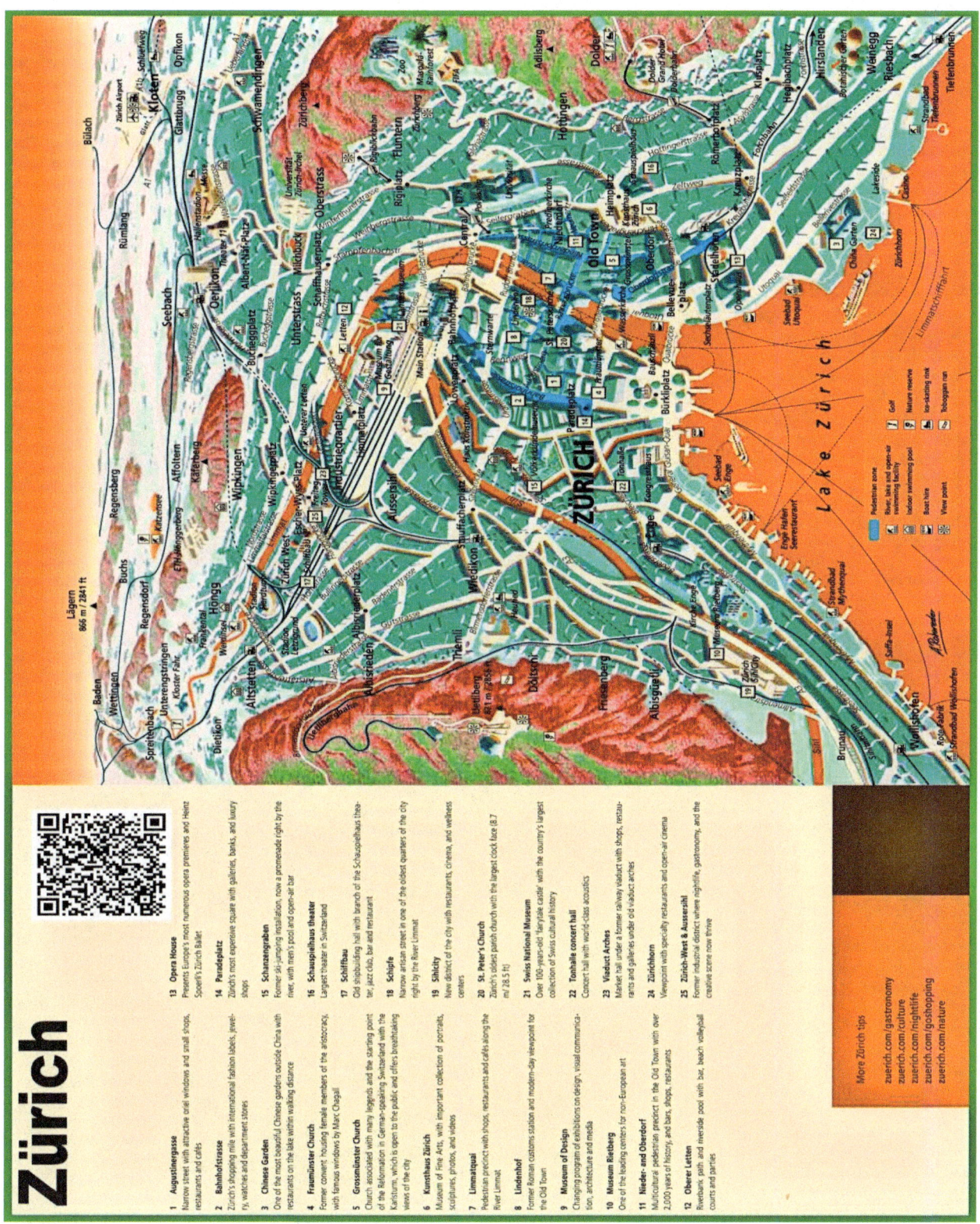

1 Augustinergasse
Narrow street with attractive oriel windows and small shops, restaurants and cafés

2 Bahnhofstrasse
Zürich's shopping mile with international fashion labels, jewelry, watches and department stores

3 Chinese Garden
One of the most beautiful Chinese gardens outside China with restaurants on the lake within walking distance

4 Fraumünster Church
Former convent housing female members of the aristocracy, with famous windows by Marc Chagall

5 Grossmünster Church
Church associated with many legends and the starting point of the Reformation in German-speaking Switzerland with the Karlsturm, which is open to the public and offers breathtaking views of the city

6 Kunsthaus Zürich
Museum of Fine Arts, with important collection of portraits, sculptures, photos, and videos

7 Limmatquai
Pedestrian precinct with shops, restaurants and cafés along the River Limmat

8 Lindenhof
Former Roman customs station and modern-day viewpoint for the Old Town

9 Museum of Design
Changing program of exhibitions on design, visual communication, architecture and media

10 Museum Rietberg
One of the leading centers for non-European art

11 Nieder- and Oberdorf
Multicultural pedestrian precinct in the Old Town with over 2,000 years of history, and bars, shops, restaurants

12 Obere Letten
Riverbank, path and riverside pool with bar, beach volleyball courts and parties

13 Opera House
Presents Europe's most numerous opera premieres and Heinz Spoerli's Zürich Ballet

14 Paradeplatz
Zürich's most expensive square with galleries, banks, and luxury shops

15 Schanzengraben
Former ski-jumping installation, now a promenade right by the river, with men's pool and open-air bar

16 Schauspielhaus theater
Largest theater in Switzerland

17 Schiffbau
Old shipbuilding hall with branch of the Schauspielhaus theater, jazz club, bar and restaurant

18 Schipfe
Narrow artisan street in one of the oldest quarters of the city right by the River Limmat

19 Sihlcity
New district of the city with restaurants, cinema, and wellness centers

20 St. Peter's Church
Zürich's oldest parish church with the largest clock face (8.7 m/28.5 ft)

21 Swiss National Museum
Over 100-years-old 'fairytale castle' with the country's largest collection of Swiss cultural history

22 Tonhalle concert hall
Concert hall with world-class acoustics

23 Viaduct Arches
Market hall under a former railway viaduct with shops, restaurants and galleries under old viaduct arches

24 Zürichhorn
Viewpoint with specialty restaurants and open-air cinema

25 Zürich-West & Ausserihl
Former industrial district where nightlife, gastronomy, and the creative scene now thrive

More Zürich tips
zuerich.com/gastronomy
zuerich.com/culture
zuerich.com/nightlife
zuerich.com/goshopping
zuerich.com/nature

Map © ontheworldmap.com - Source:
https://ontheworldmap.com/switzerland/city/zurich/zurich-sightseeing-map.jpg

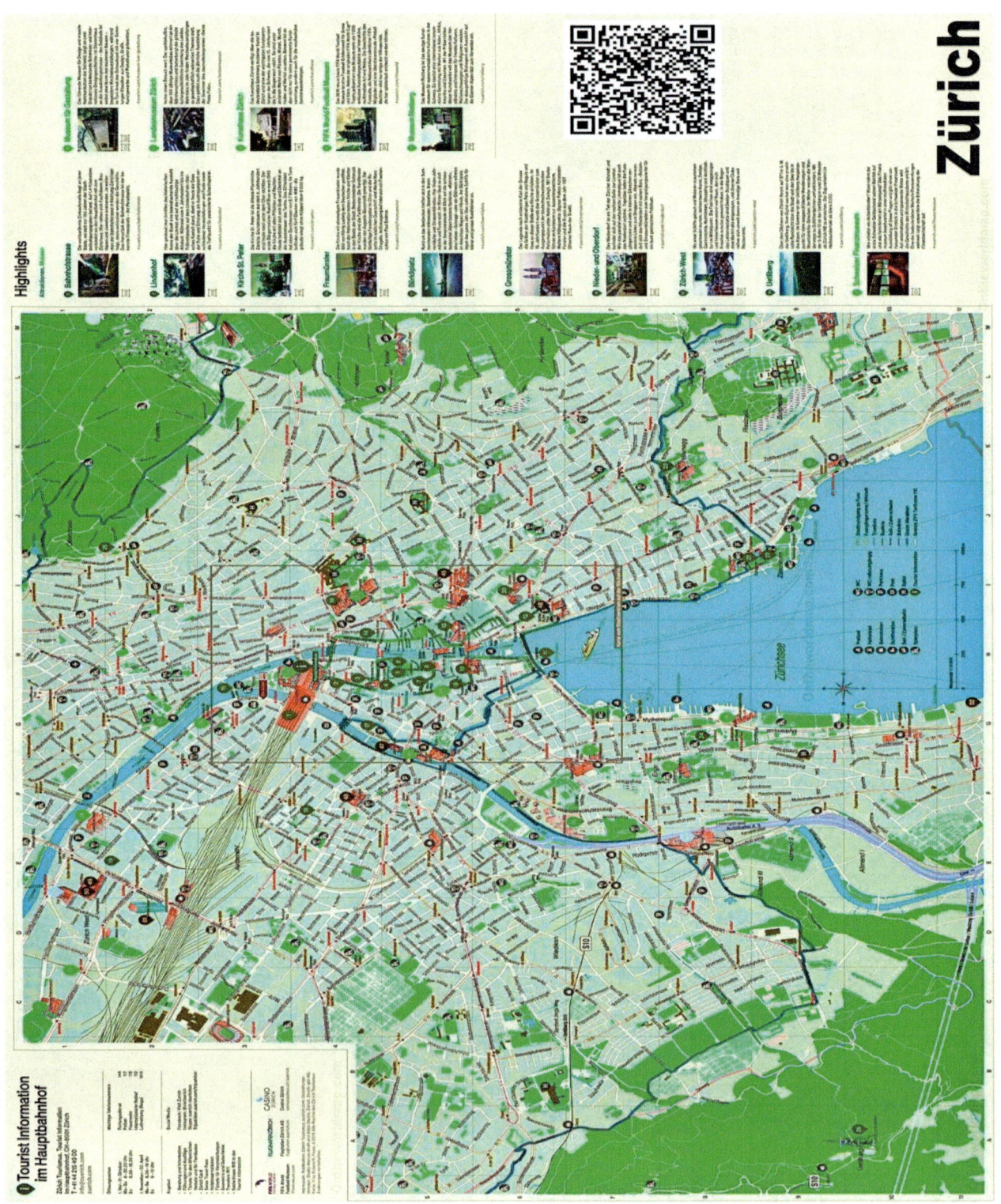

Map © ontheworldmap.com -
Source:https://ontheworldmap.com/switzerland/city/zurich/zurich-tourist-map.jpg

Chapter 2. Planning Your Trip

2.1 Best Times to Visit Zurich

Zurich is a year-round destination, with each season offering its own unique charm. The best time to visit depends on your preferences for weather, activities, and crowd levels. Here's a breakdown of what each season has to offer:

Spring (March–May)

- Weather:
  Spring in Zurich is mild and fresh, with average temperatures ranging from 8°C to 15°C (46°F to 59°F). Flowers bloom in the city's parks, and the surrounding countryside comes alive with vibrant greenery.

- Activities:

  - Stroll along Lake Zurich and enjoy the spring blossoms.
  - Visit the Botanical Garden to see exotic plants and flowers in full bloom.
  - Participate in the Sechseläuten festival in April, a traditional event featuring the burning of the "Böögg," a snowman effigy that predicts summer weather.
- Crowds:
  Spring is a shoulder season, so you can enjoy fewer tourists and better hotel rates.

Summer (June–August)

- Weather:
  Summers in Zurich are warm and sunny, with temperatures ranging from 18°C to 27°C (64°F to 81°F). Occasional rain showers provide a refreshing break from the heat.

- Activities:

  - Swim in Lake Zurich or the city's riverside pools (*Badi*).
  - Explore outdoor cafes, beer gardens, and lakeside dining spots.
  - Attend the Street Parade in August, the world's largest techno parade.
  - Hike in the surrounding mountains, such as Mount Uetliberg.
- Crowds:
  Summer is Zurich's peak tourist season, so expect higher prices and busier attractions.

Autumn (September–November)

- Weather:
  Autumn brings crisp air and stunning fall foliage. Temperatures range from 10°C to 18°C (50°F to 64°F), making it perfect for outdoor exploration.

- Activities:

  - Enjoy wine festivals in the surrounding regions, such as the Zurich Wine Festival.
  - Take a scenic boat ride on Lake Zurich to admire the autumn colors.
  - Visit the Zurich Film Festival in late September and early October.
- Crowds:
  Autumn is another shoulder season, with fewer tourists and more relaxed sightseeing.

Winter (December–February)

- Weather:
  Winters in Zurich are cold, with temperatures between -1°C and 4°C (30°F to 39°F). Snow is possible, especially in the nearby Alps, creating a magical winter wonderland.

- Activities:

  - Visit Zurich's Christmas markets, such as the one at Sechseläutenplatz or inside Zurich Main Station.
  - Go ice skating at Dolder Sports or on natural frozen ponds.
  - Use Zurich as a base for skiing or snowboarding in nearby resorts.
- Crowds:
  Winter attracts visitors for the holiday season, but it's less crowded after New Year's, offering a peaceful experience.

Recommendations Based on Interests

- For   Outdoor   Enthusiasts:
  Visit in late spring or summer for hiking, swimming, and outdoor dining.

- For   Festival   Lovers:
  Plan your trip around major events like the Sechseläuten in April or the Street Parade   in   August.

- For   Budget   Travelers:
  Consider spring or autumn for lower prices and fewer crowds.

- For   Holiday   Magic:
  December is perfect for enjoying Zurich's enchanting Christmas markets and festive atmosphere.

2.2 Getting to Zurich: Flights, Trains, and Road Trips

Zurich's central location in Europe, efficient transportation network, and proximity to major cities make it easily accessible by air, rail, or road. Here's everything you need to know to plan your journey to Zurich:

Getting to Zurich by Air

Zurich Airport (ZRH):

- Overview:
  Zurich Airport, also known as Flughafen Zürich, is Switzerland's largest and busiest airport, located just 10 km (6 miles) from the city center.
- Connectivity:
  - Direct flights connect Zurich to major cities across Europe, North America, Asia, and the Middle East.
  - Airlines like Swiss International Air Lines and Edelweiss Air use Zurich Airport as a hub.
- Airport Facilities:
  - Efficient customs and immigration process.
  - Excellent shopping and dining options.
  - Train and tram stations within the airport for quick transit to the city.

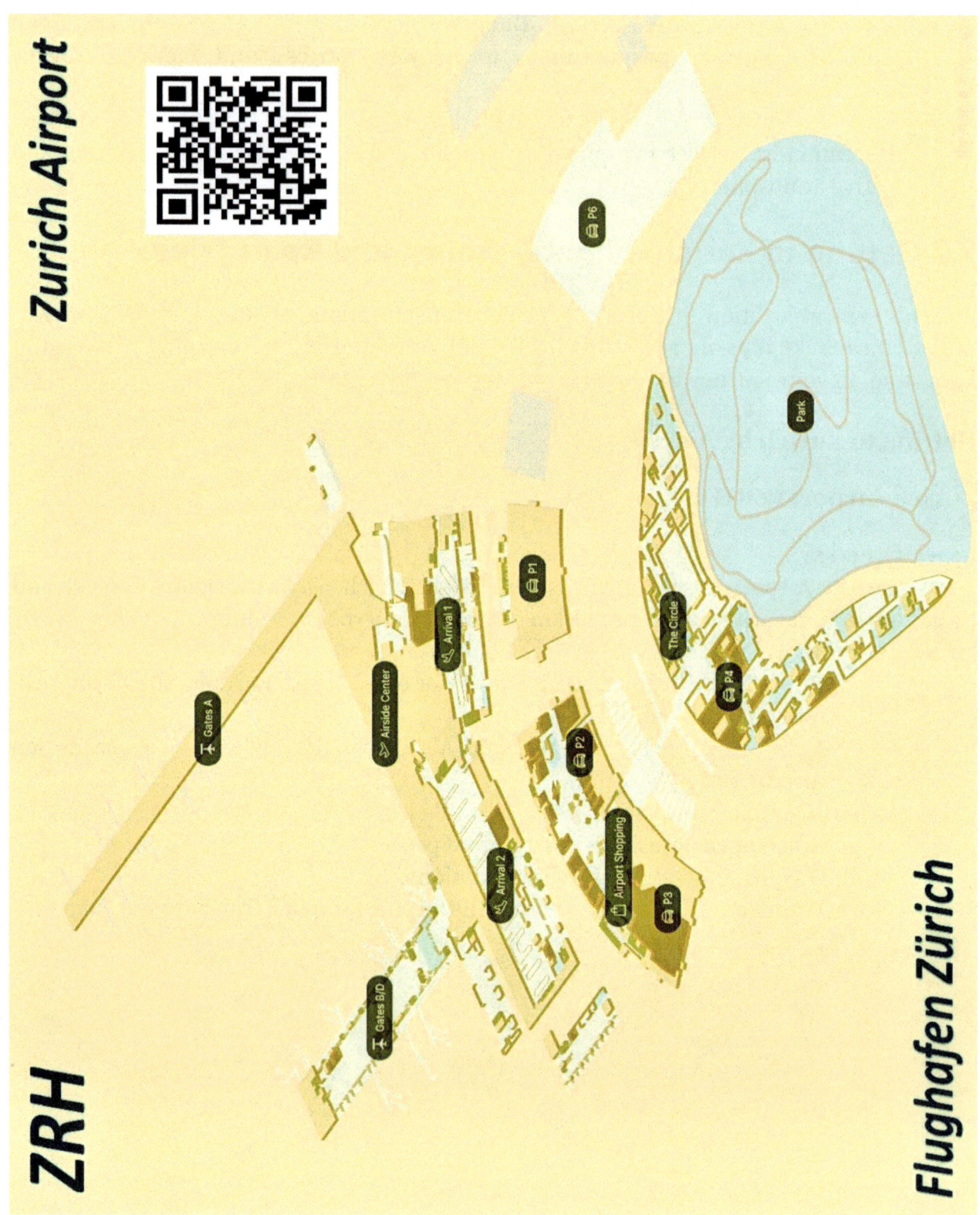

Map © ontheworldmap.com - Source:
https://ontheworldmap.com/switzerland/city/zurich/zurich-airport-map-new.jpg

Getting to the City from the Airport:

- Train:
    - Trains depart every 5–10 minutes from the airport to Zurich Hauptbahnhof (Main Station). The journey takes about 10–15 minutes.
    - Tickets cost approximately CHF 6.80 (one-way).
- Tram:
    - Tram Line 10 connects the airport to the city center in 35 minutes.
    - A great option for sightseeing en route.
- Taxi/Private Transfers:
    - Taxis are available outside the terminal, with fares around CHF 50–70 to the city center.
    - Private transfers can be pre-booked for added convenience.

Getting to Zurich by Train

Swiss Federal Railways (SBB):

- Zurich is a major hub for Switzerland's efficient and punctual train network, operated by the Swiss Federal Railways (SBB).

International Connections:

- High-speed trains connect Zurich to major European cities, including:
    - Paris: 4 hours via TGV Lyria.
    - Milan: 3.5 hours via EuroCity.
    - Munich: 4 hours via EuroCity or Nightjet.
    - Vienna: 8 hours via Railjet or Nightjet.
    - Frankfurt: 4 hours via ICE trains.

Domestic Connections:

- Zurich is well-connected to other Swiss cities:
    - Geneva: 2.5–3 hours.
    - Basel: 1 hour.
    - Lucerne: 45 minutes.
    - Interlaken: 2 hours.

Arriving at Zurich Hauptbahnhof (Main Station):

- Zurich Hauptbahnhof is located in the heart of the city and is one of Europe's busiest railway stations.

- The station features extensive facilities, including shops, restaurants, and luggage storage.

Getting to Zurich by Road

Driving to Zurich:

- Zurich is accessible by well-maintained highways from neighboring countries and within   Switzerland:

    - From Germany: Enter via the A5 or A81 highways.
    - From France: Use the A36 or A35 highways.
    - From Italy: Drive through scenic routes like the Gotthard or San Bernardino passes.
- **Tips   for   Driving   in   Zurich**:

    - Swiss highways require a vignette (toll sticker) for access, costing CHF 40 per year.
    - Parking in Zurich can be limited and expensive. Look for public parking garages or park-and-ride options.

Car Rentals:

- Rent a car if you plan to explore nearby regions or the Swiss countryside.
- Major car rental companies are available at Zurich Airport and in the city center.

Road Trips to Zurich:

- Combine Zurich with scenic routes like:
    - The Rhine Falls: Just 45 minutes by car.
    - Lake Lucerne: A 1-hour drive offering stunning views.
    - The Swiss Alps: Easily accessible for day trips.

Alternative Options: Long-Distance Buses

- Bus   Operators:
Companies like FlixBus and Eurolines offer budget-friendly options to Zurich from other European cities.
- Bus   Terminal:
Zurich's main bus terminal is located near the Hauptbahnhof, making onward connections easy.

Zürich

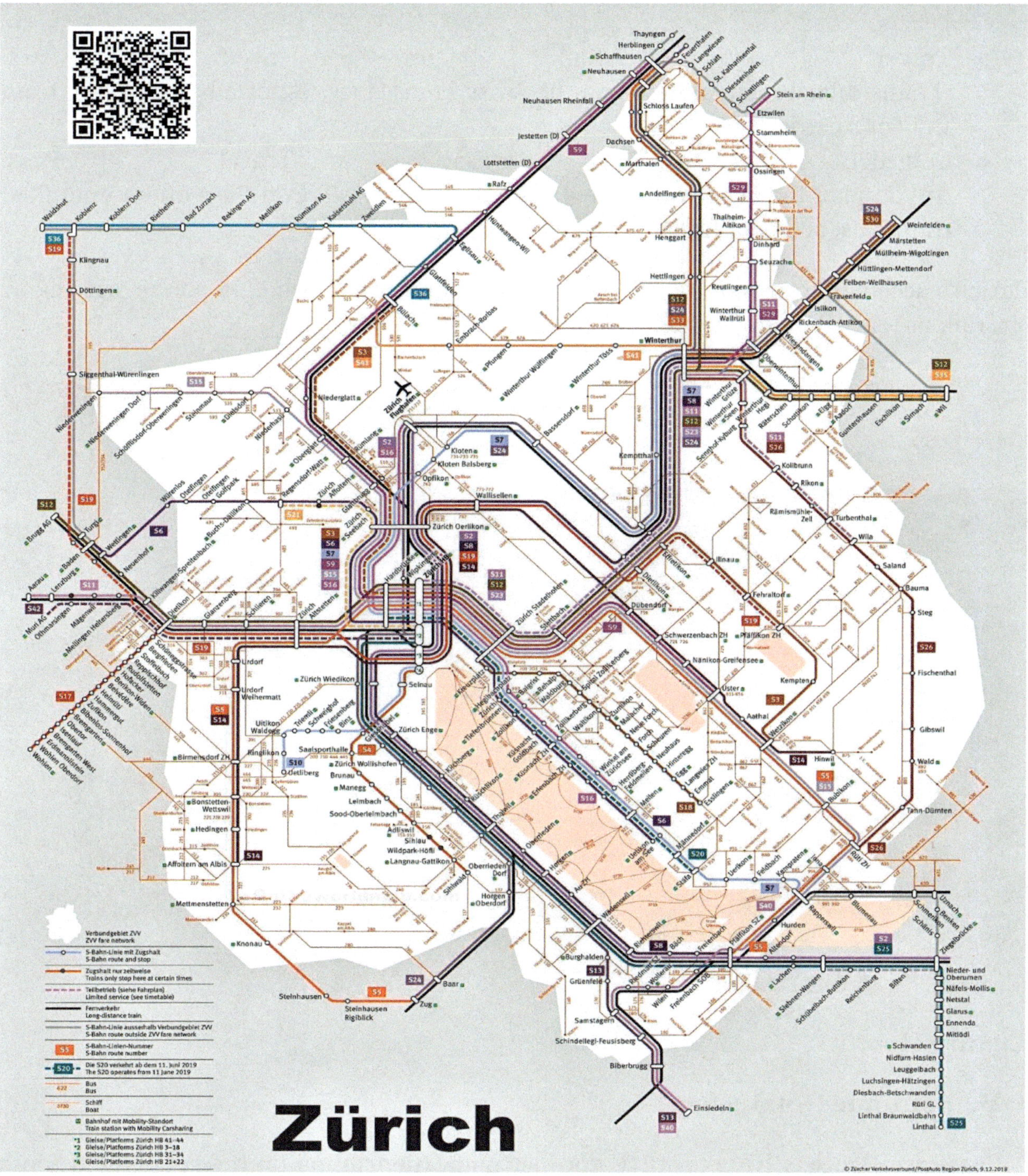

Map © ontheworldmap.com - Source:
https://ontheworldmap.com/switzerland/city/zurich/zurich-train-map.jpg

Pro Tips for Getting to Zurich

- Book   Early:
  Secure cheaper flights and train tickets by booking in advance, especially during peak seasons.
- Travel   by   Rail   for   Scenic   Views:
  Trains offer breathtaking views of Swiss landscapes, especially if arriving from Italy or Austria.
- Consider   a   Swiss   Travel   Pass:
  If you plan to travel within Switzerland, the Swiss Travel Pass offers unlimited train, bus, and boat travel, along with discounts on attractions.

Zurich's accessibility ensures a smooth start to your journey, whether you're arriving by air, rail, or road. Would you like to explore

2.3 Where to Stay: Hotels, Hostels, and Apartments for Every Budget

Luxury Hotels

1. B2 Boutique Hotel + Spa

- Price Range: CHF 250–CHF 500 per night (depending on the season and room type)
- Address: 1.2   miles   from   Zurich's   city   center
  Zurich, Güterstrasse 4, 8005 Zürich, Switzerland

- Contact: +41 44 567 67 67
- Website: www.b2boutiquehotel.ch
- Description: This stylish boutique hotel, housed in a former brewery, offers luxury rooms, an exclusive spa, and panoramic views of Zurich. It's a short walk from Zurich's main attractions like the lake and the Old Town.

2. Zurich Marriott Hotel

- Price Range: CHF 250–CHF 450 per night
- Address: Neumuehlequai 42, 8006 Zurich, Switzerland
- Contact: +41 44 360 70 00
- Website: www.marriott.com
- Description: Located by the river, this 5-star hotel offers modern amenities and exceptional views of the city and Lake Zurich. Its proximity to the train station makes it ideal for both leisure and business travelers.

Mid-Range Hotels

3. 25hours Hotel Zurich Langstrasse

- Price Range: CHF 130–CHF 220 per night
- Address: Langstrasse 150, 8004 Zurich, Switzerland
- Contact: +41 44 577 25 25
- Website: www.25hours-hotels.com
- Description: A trendy, design-forward hotel located in the Langstrasse district, known for its vibrant atmosphere and proximity to Zurich's nightlife and cultural scene. The hotel features stylish rooms and a rooftop bar.

4. Hotel Glockenhof Zurich

- Price Range: CHF 180–CHF 350 per night
- Address: Sihlstrasse 31, 8001 Zurich, Switzerland
- Contact: +41 44 225 55 55
- Website: www.glockenhof.ch
- Description: A modern yet classic hotel located in the heart of Zurich, just steps away from Bahnhofstrasse, Zurich's premier shopping street. Guests can enjoy spacious rooms, excellent dining, and easy access to the city's key attractions.

Budget Hotels and Hostels

5. Zurich Youth Hostel

- Price Range: CHF 50–CHF 120 per night (dormitory and private rooms)
- Address: Mutschellenstrasse 114, 8038 Zurich, Switzerland
- Contact: +41 44 463 57 57
- Website: www.youthhostel.ch
- Description: An affordable yet comfortable option located near Zurich's lake and a short tram ride from the city center. The hostel offers both dormitory-style rooms and private rooms, perfect for budget-conscious travelers.

Pro Tips for Choosing Accommodation in Zurich

- Book Early: Zurich is a popular tourist destination, so booking accommodations well in advance is highly recommended, especially during peak tourist seasons like summer and the Christmas holidays.
- Consider Location: Zurich's public transportation system is excellent, so if you choose to stay slightly outside the city center, it's easy to reach downtown in under 30 minutes by tram or train.
- Look for Deals: Many hotels and apartments offer special rates and discounts for early bookings or extended stays, so keep an eye out for promotions.

This selection includes accommodations for various budgets, ensuring you'll find a place that suits your needs and enhances your stay in Zurich!

2.4 What to Pack: Seasonal Essentials

Zurich offers a diverse climate throughout the year, with distinct seasons, so packing appropriately for the time of year you'll be visiting is key to ensuring comfort and enjoyment. Here's a breakdown of essential items to pack for each season to help you stay prepared.

Spring (March to May)

- Light Layers: Zurich's spring can be a mix of mild and cool days, so pack light layers that can be easily added or removed. Think long-sleeve shirts, lightweight sweaters, and cardigans.
- Rain Gear: Spring showers are common, so a compact umbrella or waterproof jacket is essential to stay dry.
- Comfortable Footwear: Since you'll likely be walking a lot to explore the city, bring comfortable shoes such as sneakers or light boots.
- Sunglasses: Though it can be rainy, there are plenty of sunny days, especially in April and May, so pack sunglasses to protect your eyes.
- Light Scarf or Shawl: Zurich's weather can still be a little chilly, so a scarf can help keep you warm in the evenings.

Summer (June to August)

- Breathable Clothing: Zurich can experience warm temperatures in summer, with highs ranging from 20°C to 30°C (68°F to 86°F), so pack light, breathable clothing like T-shirts, dresses, and shorts.
- Swimwear: The city's lakes are perfect for swimming, so don't forget to pack swimwear if you plan on enjoying the water.
- Sunscreen: The sun can be intense in the summer months, so bring high-SPF sunscreen to protect your skin from UV rays.
- Hats and Sunglasses: Hats will protect your face from the sun, and sunglasses will keep your eyes comfortable when outdoors.
- Comfortable Walking Shoes: As Zurich is a great city for exploring by foot, bring comfortable walking shoes for long days of sightseeing.

Fall (September to November)

- Layered Clothing: As temperatures drop, layers are key for fall. Think sweaters, jackets, and cardigans that can be worn over lighter clothing.
- Weatherproof Coat: The weather can be unpredictable, so pack a water-resistant coat or trench coat to stay dry on rainy days.
- Boots: As the ground can be wet and slippery, bring waterproof boots or shoes with good traction.
- Light Scarf and Gloves: As the evenings get cooler, pack a scarf and light gloves to stay comfortable.
- Portable Power Bank: Autumn days can get shorter, and you might need your phone more frequently for navigation or photos, so carry a portable charger.

Winter (December to February)

- Winter Coat: Zurich can be quite cold in winter, with temperatures often dropping below freezing. A warm, insulated coat is a must. Consider one that's water-resistant in case of snow or rain.
- Thermal Layers: Thermal underwear and long-sleeve base layers are essential for keeping warm in colder weather.
- Warm Boots: Snowfall is common, so pack waterproof, insulated boots that can handle the cold and slippery conditions.
- Heavy Gloves, Scarf, and Hat: A warm scarf, thermal gloves, and a knitted hat will help keep you cozy, especially when walking around town or near the lake.
- Moisturizer and Lip Balm: Cold weather can dry out your skin, so pack moisturizer and lip balm to keep your skin hydrated.

Year-Round Essentials

- Power Adapter: Switzerland uses the Type C and Type J plugs, and the voltage is 230V with a frequency of 50Hz, so bring a power adapter to charge your devices.
- Day Pack: A small backpack or crossbody bag is great for carrying your essentials while exploring the city.
- Reusable Water Bottle: Zurich is known for having some of the cleanest tap water in the world, so bring a reusable water bottle to stay hydrated.
- Camera/Smartphone: Whether you're capturing the city's stunning landscapes or just exploring the Old Town, make sure you bring a camera or smartphone to document your experiences.
- Travel Guide or Map: While Zurich's public transport is excellent, having a paper map or guidebook can help with navigation, especially in less touristy areas.

Packing Tips for Zurich

- Check the Weather Forecast: Before packing, always check the weather forecast for your travel dates to ensure you pack accordingly.
- Pack Light: Zurich's public transport system is efficient, but it can get crowded. A smaller suitcase or carry-on is often more convenient than large luggage.
- Waterproof Options: Since Zurich can experience sudden rainfall, bringing waterproof gear—such as a jacket, shoes, or bag—is a smart move.

With these essentials packed according to the season, you'll be well-prepared to enjoy your time in Zurich, no matter when you visit!

Chapter 3. Getting Around Zurich

3.1 Public Transport: Trams, Buses, and Trains

Zurich is known for its efficient, reliable, and extensive public transportation system, which makes getting around the city and its surrounding areas easy and convenient. Whether you're traveling within the city or to nearby attractions, Zurich's public transport system is an excellent choice for visitors. Below is a guide to the key modes of public transport in Zurich:

1. Trams: The Heart of Zurich's Public Transport

- Overview: Zurich has a well-developed tram system that is considered one of the best in the world. With over 15 tram lines, the trams are one of the fastest and most convenient ways to get around the city. Trams run frequently and cover almost all major areas, including downtown, residential neighborhoods, and key attractions.

- Operating   Hours:

  - Weekdays: Trams generally run from 5:00 AM until midnight.

- Weekends: Trams operate throughout the night, with a reduced schedule between midnight and 5:00 AM.
- Ticketing:

  - You can purchase tickets from ticket machines located at tram stops or via the SBB mobile app.
  - Ticket prices depend on the zones you travel through, and you can opt for single tickets, day passes, or multi-day passes for unlimited travel during a certain period.
  - Zurich Travel Pass: For tourists, the Zurich Travel Pass offers unlimited travel on trams, buses, and trains within the city. It's available for 24, 48, or 72 hours and includes discounts on attractions.
- Key   Tram   Lines:

  - Line 4: Takes you through the city center, passing through landmarks like Lake Zurich and Zurich's Old Town (Altstadt).
  - Line 10: Connects Zurich's airport (Zürich Flughafen) with the city center, making it a convenient option for travelers arriving or departing.

2. Buses: Connecting the City and Suburbs

- Overview: Zurich has an extensive bus network that complements the tram system, providing access to areas that are less well-served by trams. Buses are particularly useful for reaching residential neighborhoods, outlying areas, and remote locations   in   and   around   Zurich.

- Operating   Hours:

  - Like trams, buses run from early morning until midnight, with night buses available on certain routes after midnight.
  - During rush hours, buses are frequent, ensuring fast and efficient service.
- Ticketing:

  - Bus tickets can be purchased in the same manner as tram tickets, from ticket machines, the SBB app, or ZVV (Zurich Transport Network) apps.
  - Day passes and multi-ride options are available for those who plan to use public transport frequently during their stay.
- Key   Bus   Routes:

- Bus 33: Travels from Zurich's central train station to the Uetliberg Mountain, providing a scenic route to this popular hiking and sightseeing spot.
- Bus 150: Connects Zurich with the Zurich Zoo and other attractions on the eastern side of the city.

3. Trains: Connecting Zurich with Switzerland and Beyond

- Overview: Zurich's main train station, Zurich Hauptbahnhof (HB), is one of the busiest and most important transport hubs in Europe. From here, you can catch trains that connect you to other Swiss cities, as well as international destinations. Trains are ideal for longer journeys, such as trips to nearby cities, the Swiss Alps, or Lake Geneva.

- Operating Hours:

  - Zurich trains operate throughout the day, with services typically running from early morning until midnight.
  - The SBB Swiss Federal Railways (SBB) provides trains to destinations both within Zurich and across Switzerland. International trains to neighboring countries like Germany, Austria, and Italy are also available.
- Ticketing:

  - Tickets for trains can be purchased from SBB ticket counters at the train station, ticket machines, or via the SBB Mobile app.
  - Zurich Travel Pass also covers train travel within the city, including local trains (S-Bahn). For regional and international trips, you may need to buy a separate ticket depending on your destination.
- Key Routes:

  - Zurich to Lucerne: A popular day trip route, taking around 50 minutes by train.
  - Zurich to Geneva: An excellent option for those wishing to explore Switzerland's French-speaking region. The journey takes around 3 hours.
  - Zurich to Interlaken/Swiss Alps: A scenic route for travelers heading to the famous Swiss mountain towns and resorts.

4. S-Bahn (Suburban Trains): Quick Access to Outskirts

- Overview: The S-Bahn is a network of suburban trains that connects Zurich with its surrounding areas, including nearby towns and suburbs. These trains are especially useful if you're planning day trips to nearby places like Winterthur,

Rapperswil, or the Zurich Lake area.

- Operating   Hours:

    ○ The S-Bahn runs regularly throughout the day, typically from 5:00 AM to midnight, with frequent services during peak hours.
- Ticketing:

    ○ Tickets for the S-Bahn are integrated into the Zurich Transport Network (ZVV), and can be purchased at the same machines and via the same apps as those for trams and buses.

5. Tips for Using Zurich's Public Transport System

- Tickets: Always purchase your ticket before boarding. If caught without a valid ticket, you could face a hefty fine.
- Validate Tickets: When using paper tickets, you must validate them before boarding. Electronic tickets via apps like the SBB app do not require validation.
- Travel Passes: Consider purchasing the Zurich Travel Pass or Swiss Half Fare Card for cost-effective unlimited travel for tourists. These cards provide discounts on admission to popular attractions as well.
- Punctuality: Zurich's public transport is renowned for being punctual, so make sure to arrive on time at your tram, bus, or train station.

6. Alternative Transportation: Bikes, Taxis, and Boats

- Bikes: Zurich is a bike-friendly city with plenty of bike rental stations. You can rent a bike or e-scooter to explore the city at your own pace.
- Taxis: Taxis are available but are generally more expensive than public transport. You can hail them on the street or book via taxi apps.
- Boats: During the summer months, Lake Zurich boat cruises provide a scenic way to explore the lake and its surroundings. Public ferries also cross the lake regularly, offering a unique and picturesque way to get from one side of Zurich to the other.

Zurich's public transportation system is one of the most efficient and user-friendly in the world, offering an easy and affordable way to get around the city and explore the surrounding areas. Whether you're heading to the airport, sightseeing in the city center, or venturing out to nearby towns, Zurich's transport system has you covered.

3.2 Zurich on Foot: Walking-Friendly Areas and Tips

Zurich is a wonderfully walkable city, and exploring it on foot is one of the best ways to experience its charm and discover hidden gems. Whether you're strolling along the picturesque Lake Zurich, wandering through Old Town (Altstadt), or visiting green spaces, Zurich offers plenty of pedestrian-friendly areas. Here's a guide to the best places to explore by foot, along with helpful tips for walking around the city.

1. Best Walking Areas in Zurich

Old Town (Altstadt)

- Overview: Zurich's Old Town, or Altstadt, is a maze of narrow, cobblestone streets lined with medieval buildings, cozy cafes, boutiques, and galleries. This historic district is perfect for leisurely walks, offering both charming alleys and scenic viewpoints.
- Highlights:
    - Grossmünster Church: A famous Romanesque-style church with impressive views of the city.
    - Felsenegg: A hilltop offering stunning panoramic views of Zurich and Lake Zurich.
    - Niederdorf: A lively area full of cafes, restaurants, and shops. It's a great spot for a coffee or evening drinks.
- Walking Tip: The streets here are often narrow and winding, so take your time and be prepared for occasional uphill climbs.

Lake Zurich Promenade

- Overview: The Lake Zurich promenade is one of the most scenic walking paths in the city. Stretching from Zurich Opera House to Zürichhorn Park, this lakeside walkway offers beautiful views of the water, mountains, and cityscape.
- Highlights:
    - Lake Zurich: Enjoy a peaceful walk along the water's edge, with opportunities for photography, picnics, or simply relaxing.
    - Zürichhorn Park: A lush green space perfect for strolling, with sculptures, fountains, and views of the lake.
    - Badi Enge: A popular public swimming area in the summer, located along the promenade.
- Walking Tip: If you're visiting in the summer, consider stopping by one of the many lakefront cafes to cool off with a drink while enjoying the view.

Bahnhofstrasse

- Overview: Zurich's most famous shopping street, Bahnhofstrasse, is a wide, pedestrian-friendly avenue lined with high-end shops, department stores, and cafes. It runs from Zurich Main Station (HB) to Lake Zurich, offering a straightforward walk through the heart of the city.

- Highlights:
  - High-end Shopping: If you enjoy shopping, Bahnhofstrasse is home to luxury stores such as Louis Vuitton, Chanel, and Hermès.
  - Swiss Chocolatiers: Stop by renowned Swiss chocolate shops like Confiserie Lindt or Confiserie Bachmann for a taste of delicious Swiss treats.
  - Lake Zurich End: The street leads to the lake, where you can enjoy the views and perhaps continue your walk along the promenade.
- Walking Tip: The street can be quite busy, especially on weekends, so be prepared for crowds. Early mornings or weekdays are the best times for a more peaceful walk.

Kreis 5 (District 5) – The Trendy Area

- Overview: Kreis 5 is a dynamic and trendy district located near Zurich's former industrial areas. This vibrant neighborhood is home to cool cafes, creative spaces, and artistic murals, making it perfect for a relaxed walk off the beaten path.
- Highlights:
  - Zurich West: A neighborhood known for its contemporary architecture, vibrant arts scene, and trendy bars and restaurants.
  - Technopark: A hub for technology and innovation, this area features modern buildings and green spaces.
  - Viadukt: A railway viaduct that has been transformed into a shopping arcade, with boutiques, cafes, and restaurants.
- Walking Tip: The area's mix of old and new makes for an interesting walking experience. Be sure to explore the area's hidden courtyards and enjoy the contrast between old warehouses and modern developments.

Uetliberg Mountain

- Overview: For those seeking a more active walk, Uetliberg is Zurich's local mountain, offering panoramic views of the city and surrounding areas. It's a great place for a day hike or a more challenging walk, with several trails to choose from.
- Highlights:
    - Uetliberg Summit: The summit offers breathtaking views of Zurich, Lake Zurich, and the Alps. There's also a lookout tower for even better views.
    - Planet Trail: A scenic walking trail that represents the solar system with models of the planets spaced out along the route.
- Walking Tip: While the mountain is accessible by public transport, hiking up the various trails is a rewarding experience for those who enjoy nature. Make sure to bring sturdy shoes.

2. Walking Tips for Zurich

- Comfortable Footwear: Zurich is a city best explored on foot, so wearing comfortable shoes is essential, especially if you plan to walk long distances or explore cobblestone streets.
- Public Transport for Longer Distances: While walking is great for exploring the city center and local neighborhoods, Zurich also has excellent public transportation for trips to more distant attractions or neighborhoods.
- City Walks and Guided Tours: If you're interested in learning more about the city's history and culture, consider joining a walking tour. Several companies offer guided walking tours that explore Zurich's history, art, and hidden gems.
- Stay Hydrated: Zurich's weather can vary, so be sure to carry a water bottle with you, especially in warmer months. Refill it at one of Zurich's many public drinking fountains that offer clean, fresh water.
- Take Breaks: Zurich is full of cafes and scenic spots perfect for taking a break and soaking in the surroundings. Whether it's by the lake or in one of the many parks, be sure to enjoy a moment of rest during your walks.

3. Benefits of Walking in Zurich

- Discover Hidden Gems: Walking allows you to explore Zurich's lesser-known spots and hidden corners that might not be visible from a bus or tram.
- Eco-Friendly Travel: Zurich is committed to sustainability, and walking is one of the most eco-friendly ways to explore the city while minimizing your carbon footprint.
- Health Benefits: With its numerous parks and walking paths, Zurich provides a perfect environment for staying active during your travels.

Zurich's compact city center, pedestrian-friendly streets, and abundance of scenic walking routes make it an ideal destination for those who enjoy exploring on foot.

Whether you're wandering through its historic neighborhoods, strolling along the lake, or hiking in the nearby hills, walking allows you to truly experience the city at your own pace.

3.3 Bike Rentals and Cycling Routes

Cycling is a popular and eco-friendly way to explore Zurich. The city is well-equipped with bike lanes, cycling paths, and bike-sharing systems, making it easy for visitors to enjoy a leisurely ride or get around efficiently. Whether you're looking for a quick ride around the city, a scenic route along Lake Zurich, or an adventurous trail into the surrounding hills, Zurich has plenty to offer cyclists of all levels. Here's a guide to bike rentals and the best cycling routes in Zurich.

1. Bike Rentals in Zurich

Züri rollt (Bike Sharing)

- Overview: Züri rollt is Zurich's official bike-sharing program, offering free bicycles for use around the city. With a fleet of more than 200 bikes available at over 30 stations, Züri rollt is a convenient and sustainable way to explore Zurich on two wheels.
- Pricing:
  - Free for up to 4 hours.
  - After 4 hours, charges apply: CHF 2 per hour.

- Where to Rent: Bikes can be picked up and dropped off at various locations throughout the city, including near Zurich's main train station (HB) and popular tourist spots.
- How to Rent: Simply use the Züri rollt app or QR code on the bike to unlock it. You'll need to register for an account before your first ride.
- Website: [Züri rollt](#)

Lime Scooters and E-Bikes

- Overview: For a quicker, less strenuous ride, Lime offers e-scooters and e-bikes throughout Zurich. These are perfect for those who want to cover longer distances or explore areas like Kreis 5 or Zurich West without the effort of pedaling.
- Pricing:
  - E-bikes: CHF 1 to unlock + CHF 0.40 per minute of usage.
  - Scooters: CHF 1 to unlock + CHF 0.30 per minute of usage.
- Where to Rent: Lime bikes and scooters are located throughout Zurich and can be found using the Lime app. Just look for available bikes or scooters near you and unlock them via the app.
- How to Rent: Download the Lime app, create an account, locate an available bike or scooter, and unlock it by scanning the QR code.
- Website: [Lime](#)

Zurich's Bike Shops: Rent a Traditional Bike

For those who prefer a traditional bike or a longer rental period, Zurich has several bike shops offering rental services. Here are some options:

1. **Zurich Rent a Bike**

   - Overview: A reputable bike rental shop in Zurich offering a wide selection of bikes, from standard city bikes to mountain bikes, electric bikes, and family bikes.
   - Pricing:
     - City Bike: CHF 25 per day
     - E-Bike: CHF 50 per day
     - Mountain Bike: CHF 30 per day
   - Address: Zurich Rent a Bike, Sihlquai 247, 8005 Zurich
   - Contact: +41 44 271 81 51
   - Website: [Zurich Rent a Bike](#)
2. **Veloplus Zurich**

- Overview: Known for its excellent customer service, Veloplus offers a variety of bikes for rent, including road bikes, city bikes, and electric bikes.
- Pricing:
  - City Bike: CHF 25 per day
  - E-Bike: CHF 55 per day
  - Road Bike: CHF 35 per day
- Address: Veloplus Zurich, Birmensdorferstrasse 89, 8003 Zurich
- Contact: +41 44 271 85 55
- Website: Veloplus Zurich

2. Best Cycling Routes in Zurich

Zurich offers a variety of cycling routes that cater to different interests and levels of cycling experience. From leisurely rides along the lake to scenic routes in the surrounding hills, here are some of the best cycling paths in Zurich.

Lake Zurich Promenade

- Overview: One of the most scenic and popular cycling routes in Zurich, the Lake Zurich Promenade runs from Zürichhorn Park to Burkliplatz. It's a mostly flat, car-free path that takes cyclists along the shores of the lake, offering beautiful views of the water and the Alps in the distance.
- Distance: Approximately 7 km (4.3 miles).
- Difficulty: Easy
- Highlights:
  - Zürichhorn Park: A peaceful park perfect for a rest or a picnic along the lake.
  - City Views: Enjoy a picturesque ride with views of the city skyline and the snow-capped mountains.
  - Lake Zurich: Stop for a quick dip in the lake or rent a boat to paddle around.

Uetliberg Mountain: Scenic Ride to the Top

- Overview: For those seeking a more challenging ride, head to Uetliberg Mountain, Zurich's local mountain. While the summit is accessible by public transport, cycling up offers an adventurous experience with rewarding views at the top.
- Distance: Approximately 10 km from the city center to the summit.
- Difficulty: Moderate to challenging
- Highlights:
  - Uetliberg Summit: Panoramic views of Zurich, Lake Zurich, and the Alps.
  - Planet Trail: A scenic cycling route that represents the solar system, with models of the planets spread out along the path.
  - Forest Trails: Enjoy a mix of paved roads and forest trails as you ascend.

Zurich West & Viadukt: Urban Exploration

- Overview: Explore Zurich West, an up-and-coming district known for its trendy bars, restaurants, and galleries. The Viadukt — a former railway viaduct turned into a shopping arcade — offers a unique cycling experience. The route also takes you through creative spaces and murals, offering a taste of Zurich's urban culture.
- Distance: Approximately 5 km (3.1 miles).
- Difficulty: Easy to moderate
- Highlights:
  - Viadukt: Explore this iconic structure with shops, cafes, and restaurants.
  - Zurich West: Discover the modern side of Zurich with its mix of old industrial buildings and trendy spots.
  - Sihl River: Cycle along the riverbanks, enjoying both urban and natural landscapes.

Zurich to Rapperswil: Cycling the Lake Zurich Route

- Overview: For a longer and more scenic cycling route, follow the path from Zurich to Rapperswil, a charming town at the southern end of Lake Zurich. This route is ideal for cyclists who want to experience the beauty of the lake and surrounding nature.
- Distance: Approximately 25 km (15.5 miles) one-way.
- Difficulty: Moderate
- Highlights:
  - Lake Zurich: Enjoy the serene views of the lake and mountains during your ride.
  - Botmingen: Stop by this quaint village along the route for a break and refreshments.
  - Rapperswil: Explore the picturesque town with its historic castle, rose gardens, and lovely lakeside promenade.

3. Tips for Cycling in Zurich

- Helmet: While not mandatory, it's a good idea to wear a helmet for safety, especially if you're planning a longer ride or cycling in hilly areas.
- Bike Lanes: Zurich has an excellent network of dedicated bike lanes and cycle paths. Always use these lanes when cycling in the city to stay safe.
- Bike Parking: Zurich has plenty of bike racks and designated bike parking areas. Make sure to lock your bike securely when leaving it unattended.
- Weather Considerations: Check the weather forecast before heading out, as Zurich can experience sudden rain showers, particularly in the summer. Bring a rain jacket or poncho just in case.

- Cycling Etiquette: Be mindful of pedestrians and other cyclists. Always signal when turning and respect traffic signals.

Cycling in Zurich offers a fantastic way to explore the city at your own pace, with routes that suit both casual riders and more adventurous cyclists. Whether you're cruising along the lake, tackling the hills of Uetliberg, or exploring Zurich's urban neighborhoods, cycling gives you the freedom to experience the city's vibrant culture and stunning landscapes.

3.4 Navigating Zurich with Apps and Maps

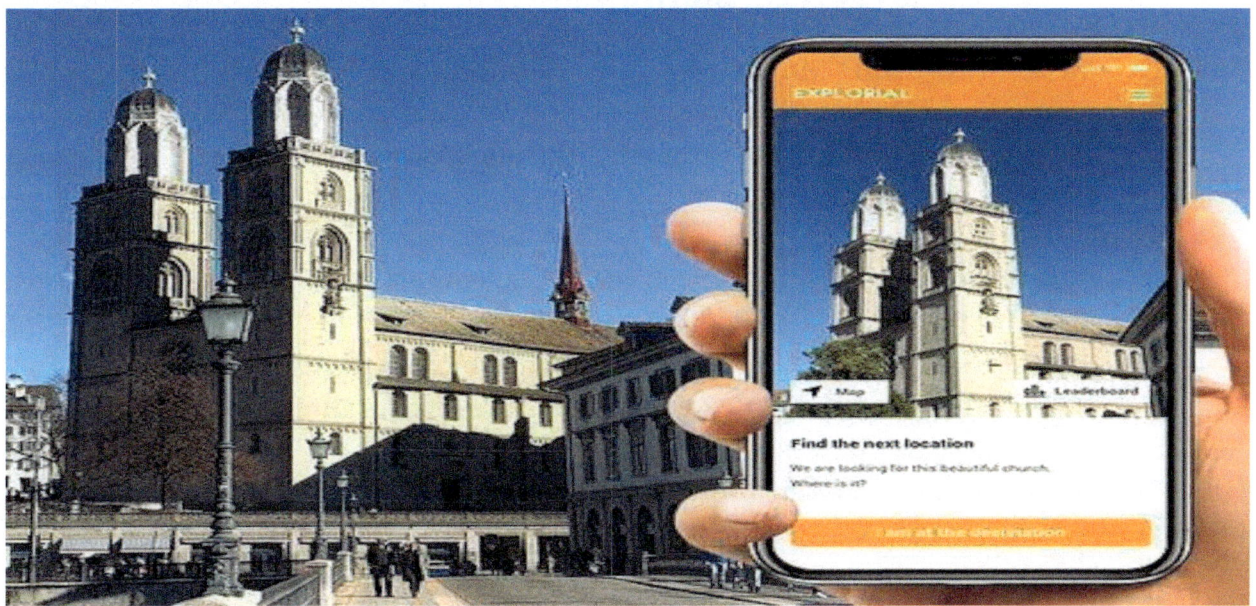

Navigating Zurich is made easier with a variety of modern apps and digital tools that help visitors explore the city efficiently. Whether you are walking, cycling, using public transportation, or driving, these apps and maps provide real-time information, clear directions, and helpful recommendations to ensure a smooth and enjoyable experience. Here's a guide to the best navigation tools for exploring Zurich in 2025.

1. City Maps and Navigation Apps

Google Maps

- Overview: Google Maps is a go-to navigation tool for most travelers and works exceptionally well in Zurich. It provides real-time directions for walking, cycling, driving, and public transport.
- Features:
  - Public transport schedules and routes for buses, trams, and trains.

- Walking and cycling routes, including bike lanes and pedestrian-friendly streets.
- Real-time traffic updates and estimated arrival times.
- Street View to preview routes or explore areas before visiting.
- Offline maps for when you don't have access to the internet.
- How to Use: Simply search for a location or enter your destination, and Google Maps will provide several navigation options with detailed directions and estimated travel times.
- Website: Google Maps

SBB Mobile App (Swiss Federal Railways)

- Overview: The SBB Mobile App is essential for travelers using public transportation in Zurich, especially the extensive train network in Switzerland. It's a perfect app for checking train and bus schedules, purchasing tickets, and getting real-time travel information.
- Features:
  - Timetable and route information for all public transport options (buses, trams, trains, and even boats).
  - Real-time departure and arrival updates to track trains and buses.
  - Ticket purchases: You can buy and store tickets directly within the app, including day passes for unlimited travel.
  - Travel Alerts: Notifications about delays, disruptions, or maintenance on public transport routes.
- How to Use: Simply enter your departure and destination stations to get detailed schedules, route options, and travel times. You can also purchase tickets and passes within the app.
- Website: SBB Mobile

Zurich City Map (Official App)

- Overview: Zurich's official City Map App is a great resource for tourists. It provides a detailed map of Zurich, including public transport routes, walking paths, bike routes, and local points of interest.
- Features:
  - Interactive city map with detailed information on sights, restaurants, public transport, and more.
  - Points of Interest: Discover local attractions, museums, parks, and shopping areas.
  - Public transport routes: Detailed tram and bus routes, including stops and departure times.

- o Search function: Easily search for locations, shops, restaurants, and other services around Zurich.
- How to Use: Download the app, and you can access the detailed map and route information to navigate Zurich with ease. The app also works offline if you need to access maps without a data connection.
- Website: [Zurich City Map]

2. Cycling and Walking Navigation Apps

Komoot

- Overview: Komoot is one of the best apps for cyclists and outdoor enthusiasts. It provides detailed route planning for cycling, hiking, and walking, including topography, difficulty levels, and points of interest along the way.
- Features:
  - o Cycling routes with elevation data, showing you the best paths and scenic rides.
  - o Offline maps so you don't need a mobile data connection when cycling or walking.
  - o Turn-by-turn navigation for a smooth and uninterrupted journey.
  - o Custom routes for bike tours or hikes, including estimated times and distances.
  - o Points of Interest: Discover local attractions, parks, cafes, and hidden gems along your journey.
- How to Use: Download Komoot, set your starting point and destination, and choose whether you want to walk, cycle, or hike. The app will provide the best route, along with voice-guided navigation.
- Website: [Komoot]

Strava

- Overview: Strava is a popular app for runners and cyclists, allowing you to track your workouts and discover routes recommended by other users in Zurich. It's ideal for those who want to explore the city on foot or bike while keeping track of their physical activity.
- Features:
  - o Route discovery: Browse or create popular cycling and running routes in Zurich.
  - o Activity tracking: Log your cycling or walking workouts and analyze your performance.
  - o Leaderboard and challenges: Compete with others and track your progress through various challenges in the city.

- Local segments: Discover the best cycling and running segments as rated by Strava users.
- How to Use: Use Strava to search for routes, track your workout performance, and get suggestions for your next run or bike ride in Zurich.
- Website: Strava

3. Local Services and Taxi Apps

Taxi Zurich

- Overview: For quick, reliable taxis in Zurich, the Taxi Zurich App is one of the best choices. It allows you to book a taxi directly from your phone, track its arrival, and pay electronically.
- Features:
    - Real-time booking: Order a taxi to your location or schedule one for later.
    - Track your ride: Track the taxi's arrival in real-time.
    - Electronic payments: Pay your fare via credit card or other digital payment methods.
    - English language: The app is available in English, making it easier for international travelers.
- How to Use: Download the app, input your location or destination, and choose your preferred taxi. The app will provide an estimated fare, and you can track the ride as it arrives.
- Website: Taxi Zurich

Uber

- Overview: Uber operates in Zurich, offering a convenient alternative to traditional taxis. It's a great option if you prefer ride-sharing services, with easy app-based booking and payment.
- Features:
    - Ride-hailing: Request an Uber ride from your location to your destination, with upfront pricing.
    - Multiple ride options: Choose from a variety of vehicles, including UberX (standard ride), UberXL (larger vehicle), and more.
    - Cashless payments: Pay via the app with your linked payment method.
    - Driver ratings: Rate drivers and see driver ratings from previous passengers.
- How to Use: Download the Uber app, set your pickup location, and choose your destination. The app will match you with an available driver, and you can track the ride as it arrives.
- Website: Uber Zurich

4. Travel and Transport Ticket Apps

ZVV Ticket App

- Overview: The ZVV Ticket App is the official app for public transport in Zurich, managed by the Zurich Public Transport Authority (ZVV). It's perfect for purchasing tickets for trams, buses, trains, and even boats within Zurich's public transportation system.
- Features:
    - Ticket purchases for single, return, and day passes for trams, buses, and trains.
    - Real-time public transport information: Check tram and bus schedules, track departures, and find routes.
    - Fares and zone information: Easily view the zones of Zurich and get details on ticket pricing.
    - Payment options: Pay via credit card or other integrated payment methods.
- How to Use: Download the app, select your ticket type (e.g., single, day pass), choose your travel zones, and pay for your ticket. You can show your digital ticket to conductors when requested.
- Website: ZVV Ticket App

Using these apps and maps will make your navigation in Zurich efficient and enjoyable, whether you're exploring the city by foot, bike, or public transport. These digital tools offer the convenience of real-time information and provide all the support needed to make the most of your Zurich experience.

Chapter 4. Top Attractions in Zurich

4.1 Old Town (Altstadt) Highlights

Zurich's Old Town, or Altstadt, is the heart of the city, rich in history and brimming with charming streets, squares, and landmarks. Wandering through the cobbled streets of Altstadt feels like stepping back in time, as you encounter medieval buildings, quaint shops, and cultural treasures. The district is divided into two parts by the Limmat River: the Left Bank (Lindenhof, University Quarter) and the Right Bank (Niederdorf, Rathaus Quarter). Below are some of the top attractions within Zurich's Altstadt, including their locations, descriptions, opening hours, prices, and websites (if applicable).

1. Grossmünster Church

- Location: Grossmünsterplatz, 8001 Zurich, Switzerland
- Description: One of Zurich's most iconic landmarks, the Grossmünster Church is a stunning Romanesque-style Protestant church that dates back to the 12th century. It is known for its impressive architecture, the striking twin towers, and its connection to the Reformation. Visitors can climb the towers for panoramic views of Zurich. Inside, you'll find remarkable stained-glass windows created by the famous artist Augusto Giacometti.
- Opening Hours:
  - Monday to Saturday: 10:00 AM - 5:00 PM
  - Sunday: Closed (except during services)
- Price: Free entry to the church.
  - Tower Entry: CHF 5.00

- Website: Grossmünster Church

2. Fraumünster Church

- Location: Münsterhof 2, 8001 Zurich, Switzerland
- Description: The Fraumünster Church, with its striking green spire, is another prominent landmark of Zurich's Old Town. Founded in the 9th century, it is famous for its breathtaking stained-glass windows designed by the artist Marc Chagall in the 20th century. The church is a must-see for art and history enthusiasts.
- Opening Hours:
    - Monday to Saturday: 10:00 AM - 5:00 PM
    - Sunday: 11:00 AM - 5:00 PM
- Price: CHF 5.00 (adults), CHF 2.00 (students)
- Website: Fraumünster Church

3. Lindenhof Hill

- Location: Lindenhof, 8001 Zurich, Switzerland

- Description: A historic hill and park, Lindenhof offers panoramic views of Zurich's Old Town, the Limmat River, and the surrounding mountains. The hill was once the site of a Roman castle and now serves as a peaceful spot for both locals and tourists to relax. It's also a great spot for photos and a calm escape from the bustling city center.
- Opening Hours: Always open
- Price: Free
- Website: None

4. Swiss National Museum (Landesmuseum Zürich)

- Location: Museumstrasse 2, 8001 Zurich, Switzerland
- Description: The Swiss National Museum offers an in-depth exploration of Swiss cultural history through an impressive collection of artifacts, artwork, and exhibitions. Located near the Hauptbahnhof (main train station), the museum's exhibitions range from the medieval era to modern times. It's housed in a beautiful castle-like building, adding to its charm and historical significance.
- Opening Hours:
  - Monday to Sunday: 10:00 AM - 5:00 PM
- Price: CHF 10.00 (adults), CHF 5.00 (students, seniors)
- Website: Swiss National Museum

5. St. Peter's Church

- Location: St. Peter-Hofstatt 1, 8001 Zurich, Switzerland
- Description: St. Peter's Church is famous for having the largest clock face in Switzerland, with a diameter of 8.7 meters. The church was built in the 13th century and is a key landmark in Zurich's Old Town. Visitors can enjoy a peaceful atmosphere inside or step outside to admire the church's towering clock and beautiful surroundings.
- Opening Hours:
    - Monday to Saturday: 10:00 AM - 5:00 PM
    - Sunday: Closed
- Price: Free
- Website: None

6. Bahnhofstrasse

- Location: Bahnhofstrasse, 8001 Zurich, Switzerland
- Description: Bahnhofstrasse is one of the world's most exclusive shopping streets, lined with high-end boutiques, luxury stores, and Swiss brands. Stretching from Zurich's main train station (Hauptbahnhof) to Lake Zurich, Bahnhofstrasse offers a mix of both modern and historical architecture, making it a perfect spot for window shopping or indulging in some retail therapy.
- Opening Hours:
    - Monday to Saturday: 10:00 AM - 7:00 PM
    - Sunday: Closed
- Price: Free to walk, shopping costs vary

- Website: Bahnhofstrasse

7. Rathaus Zurich (Zurich Town Hall)

- Location: Rathausquai, 8001 Zurich, Switzerland
- Description: The Zurich Town Hall (Rathaus) is a beautiful Renaissance building that dates back to the 14th century. It stands at the edge of the Limmat River and has been the center of Zurich's politics for centuries. The town hall is notable for its intricate wooden ceiling and charming council hall. Visitors can take guided tours or simply admire the building from the outside.
- Opening Hours:
  - Monday to Friday: 8:00 AM - 5:00 PM
  - Saturday and Sunday: Closed
- Price: Free (Guided tours available for CHF 5.00)
- Website: Rathaus Zurich

8. Kunsthaus Zurich (Zurich Art Museum)

- Location: Heimplatz 1, 8001 Zurich, Switzerland
- Description: The Kunsthaus Zurich is one of Switzerland's premier art museums, showcasing an extensive collection of European art, including works from the medieval period to contemporary pieces. Famous for its impressive collection of works by Swiss artists like Alberto Giacometti and Ferdinand Hodler, as well as international artists such as Monet, Picasso, and Van Gogh, the museum is a must-visit for art lovers.
- Opening Hours:
  - Tuesday to Sunday: 10:00 AM - 6:00 PM
  - Monday: Closed
- Price: CHF 16.00 (adults), CHF 10.00 (students, seniors)
- Website: Kunsthaus Zurich

Map © ontheworldmap.com - Source:
https://ontheworldmap.com/switzerland/city/zurich/zurich-old-town-map.jpg

4.2 Lake Zurich: Scenic Spots and Activities

Lake Zurich is one of the most iconic natural landmarks in Zurich, offering a stunning combination of picturesque views, outdoor activities, and tranquil spots to relax. Stretching over 40 kilometers in length and surrounded by mountains, parks, and quaint neighborhoods, Lake Zurich is a favorite destination for both locals and tourists. Whether you're looking to take in the scenery, engage in outdoor sports, or simply enjoy a peaceful moment by the water, Lake Zurich has something for everyone.

Here's a look at some of the top scenic spots and activities around Lake Zurich, including their locations, prices, opening hours, and websites where applicable:

1. Promenade Walks along Lake Zurich

- Location: From the city center to the eastern shore (Zürichhorn Park to Uetliberg)
- Description: The Lake Zurich Promenade is a 4-5 kilometer scenic walk that stretches along the lake, offering panoramic views of the water, the city skyline, and the Swiss Alps in the distance. The promenade is lined with lush gardens, benches, and several points of interest, making it a perfect spot for a leisurely stroll, a jog, or simply relaxing by the lake.
- Opening Hours: Always open
- Price: Free
- Website: None

2. Boat Tours on Lake Zurich

- Location: Various boarding points around the lake, including Bürkliplatz and Zürichhorn
- Description: One of the best ways to explore Lake Zurich is by taking a boat tour. There are several companies offering a range of cruises, from short 1-hour sightseeing tours to longer excursions that take you to nearby towns like Rapperswil. Some boats even offer evening dinner cruises where you can enjoy Swiss cuisine while taking in the breathtaking views.
    - Popular Boat Tour Options:
        - Zürichsee-Schifffahrtsgesellschaft (ZSG): Offers both public transport and scenic boat tours.
        - Lake Zurich Dinner Cruise: A romantic dinner option for a sunset or evening cruise on the lake.
- Opening Hours: Varies depending on the tour company and the season
- Price:
    - Public Transport Boat: CHF 2.60 - 6.00 (based on distance)
    - Sightseeing Tours: CHF 10.00 - 35.00 (varies based on the type of tour)
    - Dinner Cruises: CHF 70.00 - 100.00
- Website: ZSG Boat Tours

3. Zürichhorn Park

- Location: Zürichhorn Park, 8008 Zurich, Switzerland (on the eastern shore of the lake)

- Description: Zürichhorn Park is a serene green space that runs along the eastern edge of Lake Zurich. It offers wide lawns, shaded areas, and fantastic lake views, making it a popular spot for picnics, relaxation, or a casual walk. The park is also home to the Chinese Garden, a beautiful and peaceful space with traditional architecture, koi ponds, and lush plants.
- Opening Hours: Always open
- Price: Free
- Website: Zürichhorn Park

4. Swimming in Lake Zurich

- Location: Various bathing areas along the lake (e.g., the public swimming areas near Kusnacht and Rote Fabrik)
- Description: During the summer months, Lake Zurich is a popular destination for swimming and water sports. Several public swimming areas are open, and some of the most famous include the Kusnacht and Rote Fabrik areas. The lake's clean, clear waters and beautiful surroundings make it an ideal spot for a refreshing swim. In addition to swimming, visitors can also enjoy stand-up paddleboarding and kayaking.
- Opening Hours: Varies by location (usually summer months, May through September)
- Price: Free (except for specific private facilities and rentals)
- Website: None (swimming is free in public areas)

5. Uetliberg Mountain (Uetliberg Summit)

- Location: Uetliberg, 8143 Zurich, Switzerland (just south of the city)
- Description: For a stunning panoramic view of Lake Zurich and the surrounding city, a trip to Uetliberg Mountain is a must. From the summit, you can enjoy sweeping views of the lake, the Alps in the distance, and the entire city of Zurich. The hike to Uetliberg takes about 1-2 hours from the city center, or you can take a train directly to the top. A popular activity is to hike the Planet Trail, which is an educational walk that follows the model of the solar system.
- Opening Hours: Always open (hiking trails are open year-round)
- Price: Free to hike (train ride to the summit costs CHF 10.00 - 15.00, depending on the route)
- Website: Uetliberg Mountain

6. Boat Rentals (Kayaks, Stand-Up Paddleboards)

- Location: Various rental locations along the lake (e.g., Zürichsee-Surfer near Bürkliplatz)

- Description: For a more hands-on experience of Lake Zurich, visitors can rent kayaks, stand-up paddleboards (SUP), or even pedal boats. Renting a boat allows you to explore the lake at your own pace and discover quieter corners of the water. These rentals are available during the warmer months and often come with safety gear.
- Opening Hours:
  - Summer Months (May to September): 9:00 AM - 6:00 PM
  - Winter Months (limited availability)
- Price:
  - Kayak or Paddleboard Rental: CHF 25.00 - 40.00 for 1-2 hours
  - Pedal Boat Rental: CHF 20.00 - 30.00 per hour
- Website: Zürichsee-Surfer

7. The Chinese Garden

- Location: Zürichhorn Park, 8008 Zurich, Switzerland
- Description: Located at the edge of Zurich's Zürichhorn Park, the Chinese Garden offers an immersive cultural experience. This beautiful, traditional garden was a gift from Zurich's Chinese sister city, Kunming. It features picturesque pagodas, ponds, koi fish, and lush greenery, making it a peaceful spot to relax while enjoying the serene lake views.
- Opening Hours:
  - April to October: 10:00 AM - 6:00 PM
  - November to March: 10:00 AM - 4:00 PM
- Price: CHF 4.00 (adults), CHF 2.00 (children and students)
- Website: Chinese Garden Zurich

8. Lake Zurich Cycle Paths

- Location: Along the lake's perimeter, accessible via the city's bike lanes
- Description: The cycle paths around Lake Zurich are perfect for cycling enthusiasts looking for a leisurely ride or a more challenging route. The paths around the lake offer scenic views and access to parks, cafes, and beaches. You can rent bikes from various rental shops around the city and cycle from Zurich's city center to the neighboring villages and towns along the lake's edge.
- Opening Hours: Always open
- Price: Free to cycle; bike rentals typically cost CHF 20.00 - 40.00 per day
- Website: None (various bike rental shops in Zurich)

Lake Zurich is a vibrant destination offering a range of activities from peaceful boat rides to exciting water sports. Whether you're looking for a place to relax, enjoy a scenic view, or engage in outdoor activities, the lake area is one of the city's most inviting spots.

4.3 Bahnhofstrasse: Shopping and Architecture

Bahnhofstrasse is one of the most famous shopping streets in the world, attracting visitors with its mix of luxury boutiques, global brands, and charming cafes. Running for 1.4 kilometers from Zurich's main train station (Zürich Hauptbahnhof) to Lake Zurich, Bahnhofstrasse is a must-visit for anyone interested in Zurich's sophisticated shopping scene, its iconic architecture, and the vibrant energy of the city.

Here's a look at the top attractions along Bahnhofstrasse, including their location, prices, opening hours, and websites where applicable:

1. Luxury Shopping and Designer Stores

- Location: Bahnhofstrasse, Zurich, Switzerland (from Zürich Hauptbahnhof to Lake Zurich)
- Description: Bahnhofstrasse is renowned for its high-end shops, making it a hotspot for fashionistas and luxury lovers. The street is lined with flagship stores from top global brands like Chanel, Louis Vuitton, Gucci, and Rolex. Whether you're looking for designer clothing, luxury watches, or fine jewelry, Bahnhofstrasse is Zurich's answer to luxury shopping.
- Opening Hours:
  - Monday to Friday: 9:00 AM - 7:00 PM
  - Saturday: 9:00 AM - 6:00 PM
  - Sunday: Closed (except for a few cafes and stores near the station)
- Price: Varies by store (high-end products start from several hundred CHF)
- Website: Bahnhofstrasse Zurich

2. Historic Architecture and Landmarks

- Location: Bahnhofstrasse, Zurich, Switzerland
- Description: Along with being a prime shopping district, Bahnhofstrasse is also a treasure trove of stunning architecture. The street features a blend of classical and modern buildings, including historical landmarks like the Credit Suisse Building, Jelmoli Department Store, and the Hotel Savoy Baur en Ville. These iconic buildings showcase Zurich's rich architectural heritage, from the grandeur of the 19th century to contemporary design.
  - Key Architectural Highlights:
    - The Löwenbräu Building: A historical building that houses art galleries and cafes.
    - The University of Zurich: Although not directly on Bahnhofstrasse, it is nearby and adds a unique historical perspective.
    - The Baur Au Lac Hotel: A luxury hotel known for its exquisite neoclassical design.
- Opening Hours: Always open to walk and explore the buildings
- Price: Free (unless visiting shops or attractions within)
- Website: Zurich Architecture Guide

3. Bahnhofstrasse Fountains and Green Spaces

- Location: Bahnhofstrasse and surrounding areas
- Description: As you stroll along Bahnhofstrasse, take a moment to relax at one of the many fountains and green spaces that are scattered along the way. These pockets of nature offer a peaceful respite from the bustling shopping atmosphere and are perfect for resting during your walk. The Felsenbrunnen Fountain and

small parks near the street offer both shade and a lovely view of the surrounding historic buildings.

- Opening Hours: Always open
- Price: Free
- Website: None

4. Jelmoli - The House of Brands

- Location: Bahnhofstrasse 88, 8001 Zurich, Switzerland
- Description: Jelmoli is one of the largest and most famous department stores in Zurich. Located on Bahnhofstrasse, it offers a wide range of luxury goods, fashion, cosmetics, and Swiss watches. Jelmoli also has a unique gourmet food market and restaurants offering international cuisine, making it a great place to shop and eat. The department store has a long history and is housed in a striking architectural building, blending modern design with historic elements.
- Opening Hours:
  - Monday to Friday: 9:00 AM - 7:00 PM
  - Saturday: 9:00 AM - 6:00 PM
  - Sunday: Closed
- Price: Prices vary based on the items you purchase
- Website: Jelmoli Zurich

5. Swiss Watch Shopping

- Location: Bahnhofstrasse, Zurich, Switzerland (several stores along the street)
- Description: Zurich is known for its rich history in watchmaking, and Bahnhofstrasse is home to many of Switzerland's iconic watch brands. If you're a watch enthusiast, you'll find a wide selection of luxury Swiss watches, including Rolex, Patek Philippe, Omega, and Audemars Piguet. For many visitors, Bahnhofstrasse is the perfect destination for purchasing a high-end timepiece as a souvenir or investment.
- Opening Hours:
  - Monday to Friday: 10:00 AM - 7:00 PM
  - Saturday: 10:00 AM - 6:00 PM
  - Sunday: Closed
- Price: Starting from CHF 2,000 for entry-level Swiss watches, with prices rising significantly for high-end brands
- Website: Bahnhofstrasse Watch Shopping

6. The Hotel Savoy Baur en Ville

- Location: Bahnhofstrasse 4, 8001 Zurich, Switzerland

- Description: The Hotel Savoy Baur en Ville is a luxurious 5-star hotel located right on Bahnhofstrasse. Known for its historical significance and opulent design, the hotel has been welcoming guests for over a century. It is one of Zurich's most prestigious hotels, and its architecture is an outstanding example of Zurich's blend of classic and modern styles. While here, visitors can explore the hotel's lobby, enjoy a meal at the hotel's fine-dining restaurant, or simply appreciate its architectural beauty.
- Opening Hours: Hotel lobby and restaurant open daily
- Price: Hotel rates vary (typically starting from CHF 500+ per night)
- Website: [Hotel Savoy Baur en Ville](#)

7. The Zurich Main Station (Zürich Hauptbahnhof)

- Location: Bahnhofplatz, 8001 Zurich, Switzerland
- Description: Zurich's central train station, Zürich Hauptbahnhof, is a major transport hub and architectural landmark. Located at the start of Bahnhofstrasse, the station itself is an impressive structure with a grand hall, multiple platforms, and various shops, cafes, and restaurants. It also features a high-end underground shopping mall, The Underground Shopping Area, which is a continuation of Bahnhofstrasse below ground, offering everything from fashion boutiques to gourmet food shops.
- Opening Hours:
  - Monday to Sunday: 6:00 AM - 10:00 PM (for most stores)
  - Train Services: Operates 24/7
- Price: Free to enter; prices vary based on what you shop for
- Website: [Zurich Main Station](#)

8. Zurich Christmas Markets (Seasonal)

- Location: Bahnhofstrasse and surrounding areas, Zurich, Switzerland
- Description: If you're visiting Zurich during the holiday season, Bahnhofstrasse transforms into a winter wonderland, with Christmas markets dotting the streets. The Zurich Christmas Market held at Bahnhofstrasse and other parts of the city offers festive lights, local crafts, Christmas ornaments, and delicious seasonal treats. The market is a magical experience, perfect for shopping for unique gifts, enjoying hot mulled wine, or simply soaking up the festive atmosphere.
- Opening Hours:
  - November to December: Varies by market (usually open from 10:00 AM to 8:00 PM)
- Price: Free to visit; prices for goods vary
- Website: [Zurich Christmas Market](#)

Bahnhofstrasse is not just a shopping street, but a reflection of Zurich's elegance, luxury, and vibrant atmosphere. Whether you're visiting for high-end shopping, to admire the architectural landmarks, or to explore its diverse dining options, Bahnhofstrasse offers a unique experience that is sure to leave a lasting impression.

4.4 Swiss National Museum and Art Scene

Zurich is not only known for its modern vibe and stunning scenery but also for its rich cultural heritage. The Swiss National Museum and the city's vibrant art scene are key highlights for visitors who are passionate about history, art, and culture. From immersive exhibitions to world-class galleries, Zurich offers a wealth of artistic experiences.

1. Swiss National Museum (Landesmuseum Zürich)

- Location: Museumstrasse 2, 8001 Zurich, Switzerland

- Description: The Swiss National Museum is one of the most important cultural institutions in Switzerland, offering an insightful look into the country's history, art, and culture. Situated in a grand historic building, the museum's collections span from the Middle Ages to the present, showcasing everything from Swiss cultural artifacts, historical textiles, and furniture to contemporary art. The museum also features temporary exhibitions that explore various aspects of Swiss life and history, making it a perfect stop for anyone wanting to learn more about the country's cultural evolution.

    - Highlights:

- ■ Swiss Cultural History: Permanent exhibits offer a deep dive into the historical development of Switzerland, covering topics such as Swiss traditions, the evolution of Swiss art, and the history of everyday life.
- ■ Modern Art Exhibitions: The museum also offers rotating modern art exhibitions, often featuring contemporary Swiss artists and international figures.
- ■ The Medieval Collection: It includes relics from the early Swiss period, showcasing medieval armor, weaponry, and religious artifacts.
- ■ Children's Museum: A fun and educational space with interactive exhibits, ideal for families traveling with young children.
- Opening   Hours:

  - Monday to Sunday: 10:00 AM - 5:00 PM
  - Closed on Mondays (except during school holidays or special exhibitions)
- Price:

  - General Admission: CHF 10.00
  - Reduced Admission: CHF 5.00 (for students, seniors)
  - Free Admission: Children under 16, members, and on the first Thursday of every month (from 5:00 PM to 7:00 PM)
- Website: Swiss National Museum

2. Kunsthaus Zürich (Zurich Art Museum)

- Location: Heimplatz   1,   8001   Zurich,   Switzerland

- Description: The Kunsthaus Zürich is one of the most important art museums in Switzerland, housing an impressive collection of Swiss and international art. The museum's collection spans over 700 years of European art history, with notable works from the medieval period to contemporary pieces. Visitors will find works from the likes of Marc Chagall, Pablo Picasso, Vincent van Gogh, and Alberto Giacometti, as well as renowned Swiss artists such as Giovanni Giacometti and Ferdinand Hodler.

  - Highlights:
    - Swiss Art: The museum features one of the best collections of Swiss art from the 19th century onward, offering a unique insight into Swiss artistic movements.
    - Impressionist and Modern Art: The museum's collection includes major works from the Impressionist and modern periods, showcasing paintings, sculptures, and works on paper by renowned European and American artists.
    - Temporary Exhibitions: Kunsthaus Zürich regularly hosts rotating exhibitions that explore different facets of the art world, ranging from classic to contemporary art.
- Opening   Hours:

  - Monday to Sunday: 10:00 AM - 6:00 PM
  - Thursday Late Opening: 10:00 AM - 8:00 PM
- Price:

  - General Admission: CHF 23.00
  - Reduced Admission: CHF 18.00 (for students, seniors)
  - Free Admission: Children under 16, museum members, and on Wednesdays from 5:00 PM to 7:00 PM
- Website: Kunsthaus Zürich

3. Kunsthalle Zurich

- Location: Limmatstrasse 270, 8005 Zurich, Switzerland

- Description: Kunsthalle Zurich is an essential stop for art lovers seeking a contemporary edge. This modern art institution is dedicated to showcasing avant-garde, experimental art across various mediums, including visual art, performance, and multimedia installations. Kunsthalle Zurich offers an opportunity to explore the cutting edge of art from both emerging Swiss and international artists. Its exhibitions change frequently, giving visitors something fresh to look forward to with each visit.

- Highlights:

  - Contemporary Art Exhibitions: Kunsthalle Zurich often hosts provocative and boundary-pushing exhibitions, offering works that challenge traditional ideas of art and its role in society.
  - Collaborations and International Art: Many exhibitions feature international artists, providing a platform for global conversations in the world of contemporary art.
  - Artist Talks and Performances: The gallery often hosts events such as artist talks, live performances, and workshops, which offer deeper insight into the artistic process.

- Opening   Hours:

  - Tuesday to Sunday: 11:00 AM - 6:00 PM
  - Closed on Mondays
- Price:

  - General Admission: CHF 12.00
  - Reduced Admission: CHF 8.00 (for students, seniors)
  - Free Admission: Children under 18 and museum members
- Website: Kunsthalle Zurich

4. Museum of Design Zurich (Zürcher Hochschule der Künste)

- Location: Pfingstweidstrasse   96,   8005   Zurich,   Switzerland

- Description: The Museum of Design Zurich (also known as ZHDK), located within the Zurich University of the Arts, is a place dedicated to showcasing design, graphic arts, fashion, and applied arts. The museum explores the intersection of art and design through both permanent collections and temporary exhibitions, offering a rich variety of objects, including Swiss design classics and innovative modern works.

  - Highlights:

- Graphic Design and Typography: Known for its collection of Swiss graphic design, typography, and visual communication, this museum explores the history and impact of design on modern culture.
- Fashion and Textiles: The museum often features exhibitions on the history of fashion, textiles, and the relationship between design and everyday life.
- Design for the Digital Age: The museum also frequently showcases exhibitions that explore the impact of digital technology on design, from industrial products to virtual design.

- Opening   Hours:

  - Monday to Sunday: 10:00 AM - 5:00 PM
  - Thursday Late Opening: 10:00 AM - 8:00 PM
- Price:

  - General Admission: CHF 10.00
  - Reduced Admission: CHF 5.00 (for students, seniors)
  - Free Admission: Children under 16, museum members
- Website: Museum of Design Zurich

Chapter 5. Day Trips from Zurich

5.1 Rhine Falls: Europe's Largest Waterfall

Located just an hour's drive from Zurich, Rhine Falls is one of Switzerland's most spectacular natural attractions and the largest waterfall in Europe. This awe-inspiring natural wonder, situated near the town of Schaffhausen, offers a breathtaking sight with over 700,000 liters of water thundering over the falls every second, creating a mesmerizing display of power and beauty.

1. Overview of Rhine Falls

- Location: Schaffhausen, Switzerland (about 47 km north of Zurich)

- Description: The Rhine Falls is a majestic cascade on the Rhine River, where the water falls from a height of 23 meters (75 feet) and spans 150 meters (490 feet) in width. The falls are not only a stunning visual spectacle but also a vital part of Switzerland's natural and cultural heritage. The falls can be experienced from various viewpoints, allowing visitors to get up close to the action or enjoy a panoramic view from a distance.

  - Features:

- Viewing Platforms: Several viewing platforms offer visitors different perspectives, allowing you to feel the mist and hear the roar of the falls. The platform at the base of the falls is particularly thrilling, offering a close-up experience.
- Boat Tours: Boat tours operate during the warmer months, allowing visitors to approach the base of the falls, adding an extra thrill to the experience. You can also take a boat to the Laufen Castle situated nearby.
- Light Show: In the summer months, Rhine Falls is illuminated at night with colorful lights, making for an enchanting and magical experience.
- Nearby Castle: The nearby Laufen Castle, perched on a hill above the falls, offers panoramic views of the falls and houses a restaurant where you can enjoy local Swiss cuisine while overlooking the powerful cascade.

2. Best Time to Visit Rhine Falls

- Summer (June to August): The summer months are the most popular time to visit Rhine Falls, as the water flow is at its peak, and you can enjoy boat tours, hikes, and the illuminated evening displays. The warm weather also makes it the perfect time to explore the surrounding nature trails.
- Spring (April to May): Spring offers a quieter experience, with fewer crowds and pleasant weather, making it a great time for photography and hiking around the falls.
- Autumn (September to November): Autumn provides a stunning backdrop, with the changing foliage around the falls, offering a different perspective for visitors.
- Winter (December to March): Winter brings a serene, less crowded experience. The falls may freeze partially, creating a unique winter landscape, though the boat tours are not available during this season.

3. Activities at Rhine Falls

- Sightseeing: Enjoy the awe-inspiring views from the many platforms and observation points that offer different angles of the falls. The mist and roar of the water are a powerful experience, particularly from the closest viewing points.
- Boat Ride: A thrilling boat ride takes you to the base of the falls, where you can experience the waterfall up close, feeling the spray and hearing the thunderous sound of the water.
- Visit Laufen Castle: Explore the nearby Laufen Castle, which houses the Rhine Falls Information Centre. From the castle, you can enjoy some of the best views of the falls and the surrounding landscape.

- Hiking and Nature Walks: The surrounding area offers several walking and hiking trails that lead to beautiful viewpoints along the riverbank and through lush forests.
- Photography: The falls are a photographer's dream. Whether you're capturing the water's force from the viewing platforms or the sunset over the falls, this is a location where you can take some truly remarkable photos.

4. Getting to Rhine Falls from Zurich

- By Train: The easiest and most convenient way to reach Rhine Falls is by train from Zurich's Main Station (Hauptbahnhof). Take a train to Schaffhausen (approximately 1 hour), and from Schaffhausen station, it's a short bus or walk to the falls.
- By Car: If you prefer to drive, it's about a 45-minute journey from Zurich to Rhine Falls. The drive offers scenic views and gives you more flexibility to explore the surrounding area.
- Guided Tours: Many tour companies offer day trips from Zurich to Rhine Falls, including transport, a guide, and sometimes additional activities like a visit to Laufen Castle or other nearby attractions.

5. Practical Information

- Opening Hours: The falls are open year-round, and the viewing platforms are always accessible. The boat tours, restaurants, and other facilities are usually open from April to October, depending on the weather.
- Price:
    - General Admission (Viewing Platforms): CHF 5.00 per adult, CHF 1.00 per child (under 16)
    - Boat Tour: CHF 8.00 to CHF 12.00 for a 30-minute round trip
    - Laufen Castle Admission: CHF 5.00
- Website: <u>Rhine Falls Official Website</u>

Summary

Rhine Falls, located near Schaffhausen, is an absolute must-visit destination for anyone in Zurich. Europe's largest waterfall offers an exhilarating combination of natural beauty, historical significance, and outdoor activities. Whether you're admiring the falls from various viewpoints, taking a boat tour for an up-close experience, or exploring the nearby Laufen Castle, there's something for everyone at Rhine Falls. Easily accessible from Zurich by train or car, it's an ideal day trip that allows you to experience Switzerland's natural grandeur and peaceful surroundings, all within a short journey from the city.

5.2 Mount Uetliberg: Hiking and Panoramic Views

Just a short journey from the heart of Zurich, Mount Uetliberg offers some of the best views of the city, Lake Zurich, and the surrounding Swiss Alps. Whether you're a nature enthusiast, a photographer, or just looking to escape the city for a day, Uetliberg provides a perfect getaway with its numerous hiking trails, cycling paths, and stunning panoramic viewpoints.

1. Overview of Mount Uetliberg

- Location: Uetliberg Mountain, 8143 Zurich, Switzerland (approximately 10 km south of Zurich city center)

- Description: Rising to 869 meters (2,851 feet) above sea level, Mount Uetliberg is the highest point in Zurich, offering unparalleled views of the city, the Lake Zurich, and the distant peaks of the Swiss Alps. It's a popular destination for both locals and tourists alike, offering a range of outdoor activities including hiking, biking, and sightseeing. The summit is easily accessible by train, and once at the top, visitors are rewarded with sweeping views of the surrounding landscape.

  - Highlights:
    - Panoramic Views: From the summit, you can enjoy a 360-degree view, with the sparkling Lake Zurich to the north and the distant Swiss Alps to the south. On clear days, the views are truly breathtaking.

- Uetliberg Lookout Tower: The lookout tower at the summit provides even higher vantage points, offering panoramic views over Zurich, its surrounding countryside, and the Alps.
- Hiking Trails: Uetliberg is a paradise for outdoor lovers, with several well-marked hiking trails ranging from easy walks to more challenging routes. The Uetliberg Trail, which stretches from the mountain to the nearby Felsenegg, offers a scenic route along the ridge with beautiful views of Lake Zurich.
- Mountain Biking: The mountain also has designated biking paths for cyclists to enjoy the natural beauty while riding. Trails cater to various levels, from beginner to expert.
- Restaurants and Cafes: At the top of Uetliberg, there are several restaurants and cafes where you can relax and enjoy a meal or a drink while taking in the views. The Uetliberg Restaurant offers traditional Swiss cuisine with a view, perfect for a relaxing lunch or dinner.

2. Best Time to Visit Mount Uetliberg

- Summer (June to August): The summer months are the peak season for outdoor activities on Uetliberg, including hiking, biking, and picnicking. The trails are bustling with visitors, and the weather is typically warm and pleasant for exploring.
- Spring (April to May): Spring brings beautiful flowers and green landscapes, making it an excellent time for hiking. The weather is mild, and the trails are less crowded than in the summer.
- Autumn (September to November): The fall season is ideal for photography, as the foliage around Uetliberg turns vibrant shades of red and orange. The cooler temperatures also make hiking more comfortable.
- Winter (December to March): While winter hiking can be more challenging, Uetliberg becomes a beautiful winter wonderland, especially if there's snowfall. Some trails may be icy, but the quiet winter scenery is peaceful and serene.

3. Activities at Mount Uetliberg

- Hiking: The Uetliberg Trail, also known as the Planet Trail, is a must-do. This 4-hour trek follows the ridge of the mountain, offering sweeping views of the city and lake while passing through beautiful forests and natural landscapes. The trail ends at Felsenegg, a vantage point across the lake.
- Cycling: The mountain's biking paths offer different levels of difficulty, from easy routes to more challenging tracks. Cyclists can enjoy scenic rides through forests and up the mountain to the top, or opt for routes that lead to other viewpoints in the region.

- Panoramic Views: Take time to climb the Uetliberg Lookout Tower, which adds another 20 meters of elevation for even better views. On a clear day, the view of the Alps is particularly stunning.
- Relaxing at the Summit: After reaching the summit, visitors can unwind at the cafes or restaurants. The Uetliberg Restaurant offers a great selection of local Swiss dishes such as fondue and rösti, perfect for a meal with a view.
- Winter Sports: In winter, Uetliberg offers a more peaceful atmosphere, with cross-country skiing and tobogganing being popular activities when snow conditions allow.

4. Getting to Mount Uetliberg from Zurich

- By Train: The easiest way to get to the top of Mount Uetliberg is via the Uetliberg Railway from Zurich Hauptbahnhof (Main Station). The train ride takes about 20 minutes, and it's a scenic journey that allows you to enjoy views of Zurich's suburbs and the surrounding countryside. Once you arrive at Uetliberg Station, it's a short walk to the lookout tower and trails.
- By Car: Alternatively, you can drive to the base of the mountain, where parking is available. From there, you can either take a short walk to the summit or hike along one of the many trails.
  - Guided Tours: Several guided hiking and biking tours are available from Zurich, taking you to the summit of Uetliberg with expert guides who can explain the history and natural beauty of the area.

5. Practical Information

- Opening Hours:
  - Train Service to Uetliberg: Trains run frequently from Zurich Hauptbahnhof to Uetliberg, typically from early morning to late evening.
  - Restaurants and Cafes: Most of the restaurants at the summit are open from 9:00 AM to 10:00 PM, though hours may vary depending on the season.
- Price:
  - Train Ticket (Roundtrip): CHF 10.00 (approximately) from Zurich Hauptbahnhof to Uetliberg
  - Lookout Tower Admission: Free
  - Restaurant Prices: Depending on your choice, meals range from CHF 15.00 to CHF 35.00 for main dishes.
- Website: [Mount Uetliberg Information](#)

Summary

Mount Uetliberg offers an ideal escape from the city, providing stunning panoramic views of Zurich, Lake Zurich, and the Swiss Alps. Whether you're hiking one of the many trails, cycling through the forests, or simply relaxing at the summit with a meal and a view, Mount Uetliberg is a must-visit destination for anyone looking to experience the natural beauty of Zurich. Accessible by train, it's a quick and easy day trip from the city that rewards visitors with some of the best outdoor activities and scenic landscapes in the region.

5.3 Lucerne and Mount Pilatus

Located just an hour away from Zurich, Lucerne is one of Switzerland's most picturesque cities, nestled between the stunning Lake Lucerne and the towering peaks of the Swiss Alps. A visit to Lucerne offers a delightful blend of history, culture, and natural beauty. For those seeking adventure and panoramic views, a trip to Mount Pilatus—a majestic peak overlooking Lucerne—is a must. Whether you're interested in hiking, taking a scenic cable car ride, or simply soaking in the views, this day trip promises to be unforgettable.

1. Overview of Lucerne and Mount Pilatus

- Location: Lucerne, Switzerland (approximately 52 km from Zurich)

- Description: Lucerne is a charming city known for its preserved medieval architecture, stunning lakeside setting, and proximity to the Swiss Alps. It's famous for landmarks like the Chapel Bridge (Kapellbrücke), Lion Monument, and

Old Town, making it a cultural and historical hub. Just outside Lucerne lies Mount Pilatus, a towering peak offering awe-inspiring views of Lucerne and the surrounding alpine landscapes.

- Lucerne Highlights:
  - Lake Lucerne: The lake, surrounded by mountains, offers boat cruises, swimming spots, and scenic walks along its shores.
  - Chapel Bridge and Water Tower: This iconic wooden bridge, dating back to the 14th century, is adorned with paintings that depict Lucerne's history.
  - Old Town: The city's Old Town is a maze of narrow cobbled streets, colorful buildings, and charming squares.
  - Lion Monument: A striking sculpture that honors Swiss Guards who were killed during the French Revolution.

2. Mount Pilatus: The Peak Above Lucerne

- Location: Mount Pilatus, Switzerland (altitude: 2,132 meters / 7,000 feet)

- Description: Known as the "Dragon Mountain" due to the local legend of a dragon inhabiting the peak, Mount Pilatus is an iconic mountain offering some of the best panoramic views in Switzerland. Visitors can reach the top by a combination of the Pilatus Railway, the world's steepest cogwheel railway, or by cable car. Once at the summit, visitors are treated to spectacular views of the city of Lucerne, Lake Lucerne, and the Alps.

  - Features:
    - Cogwheel Railway (Pilatusbahn): This historic railway climbs the mountain from Alpnachstad to the summit of Pilatus, offering stunning views along the way. It's a thrilling experience, as the railway climbs at a gradient of up to 48%.
    - Cable Cars and Aerial Cableway: Alternatively, visitors can take the cable car from Kriens, which offers a different scenic experience, connecting the base of the mountain to the summit.
    - Panoramic Views: From the top, visitors can enjoy breathtaking views of the surrounding mountains, including the Rigi, Eiger, and Matterhorn.
    - Hiking Trails: For hiking enthusiasts, there are several scenic trails around the mountain, ranging from easy walks to more challenging routes, including a trail leading to the summit from Kriens.

3. Best Time to Visit Lucerne and Mount Pilatus

- Summer (June to August): The summer months offer the best weather for outdoor activities, including hiking and boat cruises on Lake Lucerne. It's also the prime time to visit the mountain, as the cogwheel railway and cable cars operate daily.
- Spring (April to May): Spring is a beautiful time to visit Lucerne and Mount Pilatus, as the surrounding nature begins to bloom. While some higher-altitude trails may still have snow, the weather is mild, and crowds are fewer.
- Autumn (September to November): Fall is another excellent time to visit, as the surrounding landscape is painted with autumn colors. The weather is still pleasant for hiking, and the crowds are generally thinner than in the summer.
- Winter (December to March): Winter transforms Mount Pilatus into a snowy wonderland, ideal for snowshoeing and skiing. However, the weather can be chilly, and the lower base areas of Lucerne may experience some snowfall.

4. Activities in Lucerne and Mount Pilatus

- Lucerne City Exploration:
  - Chapel Bridge and Old Town: Stroll through the charming Old Town and visit landmarks like the Chapel Bridge, which is the oldest wooden bridge in Europe.
  - Lion Monument: The Lion Monument is a must-see, commemorating Swiss Guards who died during the French Revolution.
  - Boat Cruise on Lake Lucerne: Take a relaxing boat ride on the lake, enjoying views of the city and the surrounding mountains.
- Mount Pilatus Activities:
  - Cogwheel Railway and Cable Car Ride: Experience the thrilling journey to the top of Mount Pilatus via the Pilatus Railway or cable car.
  - Hiking and Outdoor Exploration: Once at the summit, explore the hiking trails around Mount Pilatus. Trails vary in difficulty, offering something for all levels of hikers.
  - Panoramic Views: Don't miss the incredible 360-degree views of Lucerne, Lake Lucerne, and the Alps from the top of Pilatus.
  - Pilatus Panorama Restaurant: After reaching the summit, enjoy a meal at the Pilatus Panorama Restaurant, offering Swiss specialties with a view.
  - Winter Sports: In the winter months, Mount Pilatus is a popular spot for snowshoeing, skiing, and tobogganing, making it a year-round destination for outdoor enthusiasts.

5. Getting to Lucerne and Mount Pilatus

- **By Train:** Lucerne is easily accessible by train from Zurich's Main Station (Hauptbahnhof). The train ride takes about 50 minutes, offering scenic views of the Swiss countryside. Once in Lucerne, you can reach the base of Mount Pilatus by local public transportation or taxi.
- **By Boat and Train:** During the warmer months, a scenic boat ride from Lucerne to Alpnachstad (the departure point for the Pilatus Railway) is a popular way to start the journey.
- **By Car:** Lucerne is also easily accessible by car, and there is ample parking available in the city and at the base of Mount Pilatus.
- **By Cable Car:** From Lucerne, take a bus or tram to Kriens, where you can board the aerial cableway to the summit of Mount Pilatus.

6. Practical Information

- Opening Hours:
  - Pilatus Railway: Operates from May to November. The exact times vary, so it's best to check the schedule in advance.
  - Cable Cars: Open year-round, with operations depending on weather conditions.
  - Mount Pilatus Summit Restaurants: Open daily, with varying hours based on the season.
- Price:
  - Pilatus Cogwheel Railway (Roundtrip): CHF 72.00 for adults, CHF 36.00 for children (single trip: CHF 37.00)
  - Cable Car (Roundtrip from Kriens): CHF 38.00 for adults, CHF 19.00 for children
  - Boat Ride (Lucerne to Alpnachstad): CHF 25.00 for adults, CHF 12.00 for children
  - Hiking Access: Free (unless using the cable car or cogwheel train)
- Website: Pilatus Website

Summary

Lucerne and Mount Pilatus offer a spectacular combination of city charm and alpine adventure. The city itself is rich in culture and history, with must-see landmarks like the Chapel Bridge, Lion Monument, and a scenic boat cruise on Lake Lucerne. Just outside Lucerne, Mount Pilatus offers incredible views, thrilling outdoor activities, and access to Switzerland's stunning landscapes. Whether you are taking a scenic ride on the cogwheel railway, hiking through alpine meadows, or enjoying panoramic views from the summit, a trip to Lucerne and Mount Pilatus is a perfect day trip from Zurich. The region is accessible year-round, with activities suited to all seasons, making it a must-visit destination for nature lovers and adventure seekers alike.

5.4 Jungfraujoch: The Top of Europe

Known as the Top of Europe, Jungfraujoch is one of the most iconic and breathtaking destinations in Switzerland. Located in the Bernese Alps, it is the highest railway station in Europe at an elevation of 3,454 meters (11,332 feet) above sea level. Accessible year-round via a scenic and adventurous train ride, Jungfraujoch offers visitors a unique experience of glaciers, snow-capped peaks, and stunning panoramic views of the Swiss Alps. It is a must-visit day trip for anyone staying in Zurich looking for an unforgettable alpine experience.

1. Overview of Jungfraujoch

- Location: Jungfraujoch, Bernese Oberland, Switzerland (approximately 130 km from Zurich)

- Description: Jungfraujoch is a high-altitude mountain pass located between two towering peaks, the Jungfrau and the Mönch, in the Bernese Alps. The region is famous for its incredible views, glaciers, and the fact that it is the highest railway station in Europe. Visitors can take a scenic cogwheel train ride to the top, passing through tunnels carved into the mountain, and then explore the Ice Palace, Sphinx Observatory, and panoramic terraces.

  - Key Features:

- Sphinx Observatory: The Sphinx Observatory is an iconic structure offering 360-degree views of the surrounding snow-capped peaks, glaciers, and valleys.
- Ice Palace: An impressive ice sculpture gallery carved into the glacier, showcasing intricate ice carvings of animals and alpine themes.
- Panorama Terrace: The observation deck at Jungfraujoch provides breathtaking views of the Aletsch Glacier, the longest glacier in the Alps, and surrounding peaks.
- Jungfrau Glacier: The glacier is a remarkable sight and can be explored through the various hiking trails that begin at the Jungfraujoch summit.

2. Best Time to Visit Jungfraujoch

- Summer (June to August): Summer is the peak season for visiting Jungfraujoch, as the weather is mild and visitors can enjoy walking along the glacier and exploring the outdoor terraces. The train journey to the top is most popular during this time.
- Spring (April to May): Spring offers slightly fewer tourists, and although there may still be snow on the ground, the weather is typically clear, making it a good time for outdoor activities.
- Autumn (September to November): Autumn is quieter and offers crisp weather, perfect for a peaceful experience. The surrounding peaks are often more visible with fewer tourists than in the summer.
- Winter (December to March): Winter transforms Jungfraujoch into a winter wonderland, ideal for snow sports. The cold temperatures make it ideal for snowshoeing and exploring the glaciers, though the weather can be challenging.

3. Activities at Jungfraujoch

- Sphinx Observatory: Take in breathtaking 360-degree views of the Aletsch Glacier, the longest glacier in the Alps, and surrounding peaks such as the Eiger, Mönch, and Jungfrau.
- Ice Palace: Explore the Ice Palace, an artfully carved tunnel inside the glacier filled with impressive ice sculptures, ranging from intricate animals to alpine scenes.
- Panorama Terrace: Enjoy an elevated, panoramic view of the mountains and glaciers at the Panorama Terrace. In winter, the terrace becomes a prime spot for snow activities.
- Jungfrau Glacier Trail: Visitors can take guided tours along the glacier or walk on the Jungfrau Glacier Trail to explore its majestic ice formations.
- Alpine Activities: You can also enjoy activities like snow tubing, sledding, or skiing in winter, and hiking or snowshoeing in the warmer months.

4. How to Get to Jungfraujoch

- By Train: The journey to Jungfraujoch begins with a train ride from Zurich Hauptbahnhof (Main Station). From Zurich, take a train to Interlaken (approximately 2 hours) and then connect to the Grindelwald or Lauterbrunnen stations. From there, take the famous Jungfrau Railway, a cogwheel train that climbs to the summit of Jungfraujoch.
  - Train Journey Duration: The entire journey from Zurich to Jungfraujoch takes around 4 hours one-way.
  - Jungfrau Railway Tickets: The roundtrip cost from Zurich to Jungfraujoch is around CHF 100–150, depending on the chosen route and class of service.
- By Car: While driving to Jungfraujoch isn't possible due to the steep and snowy terrain, visitors can drive to nearby towns like Grindelwald or Lauterbrunnen and then continue by train to the Jungfraujoch.

5. Ticket Prices

- Train Tickets (Zurich to Jungfraujoch):
  - Adult (Roundtrip): CHF 100–150 (price varies based on route, class, and season)
  - Children (Roundtrip): CHF 30–50
  - Swiss Travel Pass Holders: Discounts available, generally about 25% off the regular fare.
- Jungfraujoch Admission (Top of Europe):
  - Sphinx Observatory and Ice Palace Access: Included with the train ticket to Jungfraujoch.
  - Additional Activities: Some activities such as guided glacier walks may require extra fees, around CHF 50–100 per person.

6. Practical Information

- Opening   Hours:

  - Jungfraujoch: Open year-round, with the train service running daily. The operating hours for the Jungfrau Railway are typically from 8:00 AM to 4:30 PM, with some seasonal variations.
  - Sphinx Observatory: Open daily, with extended hours in the summer months.
  - Ice Palace: Open daily, included with the Jungfraujoch ticket.

- What   to   Bring:
  - Warm clothing is essential, even in summer, due to the cold and wind at the summit.
  - Sunglasses and sunscreen are recommended, as the sun can be strong at such high altitudes.
  - Sturdy shoes for walking on the glacier if you plan to explore the ice trail or do snowshoeing.
- Website: Jungfraujoch - Top of Europe

Summary

A trip to Jungfraujoch, the Top of Europe, is a once-in-a-lifetime experience for nature lovers, adventure seekers, and those seeking the most spectacular views of the Swiss Alps. At over 3,400 meters, this breathtaking mountain pass offers an unforgettable adventure, complete with the Sphinx Observatory, the Ice Palace, and panoramic vistas of glaciers and peaks. The journey via the famous Jungfrau Railway is an experience in itself, with stunning alpine landscapes unfolding as you ascend to the summit. Whether visiting for hiking, skiing, or simply enjoying the views, Jungfraujoch is a must-see day trip from Zurich, offering activities and experiences suitable for all seasons.

Chapter 6. Cultural Experiences

6.1 Zurich's Festivals and Events in 2025

Zurich, as Switzerland's cultural and financial hub, offers a dynamic range of festivals and events throughout the year. From arts and music to food and traditions, the city has something for every traveler, whether you're seeking immersive cultural experiences or simply enjoying the lively atmosphere. The following is a list of some of the most anticipated festivals and events in Zurich in 2025.

1. Zurich Film Festival (ZFF)

- Location: Various venues across Zurich, including theaters like Kino Corso and Zurich Opernhaus.
- Dates: Typically held in late September to early October.
- Description: The Zurich Film Festival is one of Switzerland's most prestigious film festivals, attracting filmmakers, critics, and cinephiles from around the world. The festival features a diverse selection of films, ranging from international blockbusters to independent works. You can expect red carpet events, screenings, and an opportunity to meet the stars and directors behind the films. The ZFF also holds panels and discussions related to the film industry.
- Website: Zurich Film Festival

- Price: Tickets typically range from CHF 15 to CHF 30 per screening.

2. Street Parade

- Location: Lake Zurich and surrounding streets.
- Dates: Typically held in mid-August.
- Description: One of the world's largest electronic dance music festivals, Street Parade turns Zurich into a vibrant celebration of music, art, and freedom. Thousands of electronic music enthusiasts from across the globe gather to enjoy performances by top DJs, dance in the streets, and celebrate unity and diversity. The parade itself features large, colorful floats carrying sound systems and artists, making for an unforgettable visual and auditory experience.
- Website: Street Parade
- Price: Free to attend, but VIP areas and special events may charge an entry fee.

3. Zurich Art Weekend

- Location: Art galleries, museums, and cultural spaces across Zurich.
- Dates: Usually held in June.
- Description: Zurich Art Weekend is a major event for art lovers, offering a chance to experience the city's thriving art scene. Over the course of the weekend, local galleries, museums, and cultural spaces open their doors for special exhibitions, gallery tours, and artist talks. It's a perfect opportunity to explore Zurich's contemporary art landscape, featuring works by both established and emerging artists.
- Website: Zurich Art Weekend
- Price: Many events are free, while others may require tickets or registration in advance.

4. Sechseläuten

- Location: Parade grounds in Zurich's city center, particularly Bellevue Square and Lindenhof.
- Dates: The Sunday following Easter (April 13 in 2025).
- Description: Sechseläuten is a centuries-old tradition marking the end of winter and the beginning of spring. The highlight of the festival is the burning of the Böögg, a large snowman effigy representing winter. The event features a grand parade with participants dressed in historical costumes, showcasing Zurich's heritage. The Böögg's head is filled with fireworks, and its burning is said to predict the summer weather — the faster it burns, the hotter the summer will be.
- Website: Sechseläuten
- Price: Free to attend.

5. Zurich Pride

- Location: Parade route through Zurich's city center, culminating at Helmhaus near Lake Zurich.
- Dates: Typically held in June.
- Description: Zurich Pride is the largest LGBTQ+ event in Switzerland, promoting equality and acceptance. The event kicks off with a parade through the heart of Zurich, followed by celebrations at the festival grounds near Lake Zurich. Expect vibrant costumes, live music, dance performances, and a strong sense of solidarity. Zurich Pride is a powerful statement for diversity and an inclusive society.
- Website: Zurich Pride
- Price: Free to attend, but VIP packages and parties may require tickets.

6. Zurich Christmas Markets

- Location: Various locations, including Zurich Hauptbahnhof (Main Station) and Werdmühleplatz.
- Dates: Late November to December 24.
- Description: Zurich's Christmas markets are a magical way to get into the holiday spirit. The Christkindlimarkt at Zurich Hauptbahnhof is one of the largest indoor Christmas markets in Europe, featuring hundreds of stalls selling handmade crafts, delicious Swiss treats, and unique gifts. The Werdmühleplatz market focuses on high-quality artisanal goods, while other smaller markets can be found throughout the city. The aroma of mulled wine and roasted chestnuts fills the air as you explore these festive bazaars.
- Website: Zurich Christmas Markets
- Price: Free to visit, but items for sale and food/drinks range in price.

7. Zurich Openair

- Location: Zurich Rümlang, near Zurich Airport.
- Dates: Typically held in August.
- Description: Zurich Openair is a popular music festival that brings together top international and local bands across a variety of genres, including rock, pop, electronic, and indie music. The festival is held in an open-air venue surrounded by natural scenery, making it a perfect summer getaway for music lovers. With an energetic atmosphere and multiple stages, the festival is one of the highlights of Zurich's summer events calendar.
- Website: Zurich Openair
- Price: Single-day tickets range from CHF 90 to CHF 130, with weekend passes available.

8. Zurich Opera House (Opernhaus Zürich) Performances

- Location: Falkenstrasse 1, 8008 Zurich.
- Dates: Year-round, with performances most evenings.
- Description: The Zurich Opera House is one of Europe's leading venues for opera, ballet, and classical music performances. In 2025, it will host a range of operatic productions, symphony concerts, and ballet performances, including works by renowned composers such as Mozart, Wagner, and Tchaikovsky. The stunning architecture and world-class acoustics make attending a performance here a must-do cultural experience.
- Website: Zurich Opera House
- Price: Tickets typically range from CHF 40 to CHF 250, depending on the performance and seating.

Summary

Zurich is a city that embraces cultural diversity and celebrates creativity throughout the year. Whether you're visiting for Zurich Film Festival, the vibrant Street Parade, or the centuries-old traditions of Sechseläuten, there's no shortage of exciting events to experience in 2025. From music and dance to art and history, Zurich's festivals reflect its rich cultural heritage and modern spirit, offering something for everyone to enjoy. Make sure to plan your visit around one of these amazing events to make the most of your trip to Zurich.

6.2 Theatre, Opera, and Live Music in Zurich

Zurich is a vibrant cultural hub, renowned for its lively theatre scene, world-class opera performances, and diverse live music venues. Whether you're a fan of classical music, contemporary theatre, or live gigs in intimate venues, Zurich offers a wide range of performances and events to suit all tastes. Here's a look at some of the top venues and experiences for theatre, opera, and live music in Zurich:

1. Zurich Opera House (Opernhaus Zürich)

- Location: Falkenstrasse 1, 8008 Zurich
- Price: Ticket prices range from CHF 20 to CHF 250, depending on the performance and seat selection.
- Opening Hours:
    - Box office: Monday to Friday, 10 AM to 6 PM
    - Performance times: Vary by show (typically 7:30 PM for evening performances)
- Description: The Zurich Opera House is one of Europe's leading opera houses and a key venue for classical music and ballet performances. It hosts a wide variety of productions, from classical operas by composers like Mozart and Verdi to contemporary works. The opera house also features a strong ballet program and concert performances. The building itself is a stunning blend of historic and modern architectural elements, making it a must-visit for lovers of high culture.
- Website: Zurich Opera House

2. Schauspielhaus Zürich (Zurich Theatre)

- Location: Pfauenstrasse 6, 8001 Zurich
- Price: Tickets typically range from CHF 25 to CHF 90, depending on the performance and seating.
- Opening Hours:
    - Box office: Monday to Saturday, 10 AM to 6 PM
    - Performance times: Vary by show (usually evening performances at 7:30 PM)
- Description: Schauspielhaus Zürich is one of the most important theatres in Switzerland, offering a dynamic and diverse lineup of performances that include contemporary plays, classical theatre, and experimental works. The theatre also focuses on international productions, providing a platform for cutting-edge European and global theatre. The venue's innovative programming and intimate setting make it a top choice for theatre lovers in Zurich.
- Website: Schauspielhaus Zürich

3. Tonhalle Zürich (Tonhalle Orchestra Zurich)

- Location: Claridenstrasse 7, 8001 Zurich
- Price: Tickets typically range from CHF 30 to CHF 120, depending on the concert and seating.
- Opening Hours:
  - Box office: Monday to Friday, 10 AM to 6 PM
  - Concert times: Performances typically start at 8 PM, with occasional matinees at 4 PM
- Description: The Tonhalle Zürich is one of the best venues for classical music in Zurich, home to the prestigious Tonhalle Orchestra Zurich. The orchestra, conducted by renowned maestros, performs a broad repertoire ranging from classical masterpieces to contemporary works. The acoustics of the concert hall are world-class, ensuring an exceptional experience for concertgoers. The venue also hosts chamber music performances, recitals, and occasionally crossover music genres.
- Website: Tonhalle Zürich

4. Moods Jazz Club

- Location: Kraftstrasse 6, 8004 Zurich
- Price: Tickets typically range from CHF 25 to CHF 50, depending on the artist and performance.
- Opening Hours:
  - Monday to Saturday: 7:30 PM to late
  - Closed on Sundays
- Description: Moods is one of Zurich's top live music venues, known for its intimate setting and world-class jazz performances. This legendary jazz club hosts a variety of concerts, ranging from local talent to international jazz greats. In addition to jazz, Moods also features performances from other genres such as blues, soul, and funk. The club has a vibrant atmosphere and is a perfect spot for music lovers to enjoy an evening of live tunes.
- Website: Moods Jazz Club

5. Papiersaal

- Location: Pfingstweidstrasse 16, 8005 Zurich
- Price: Tickets typically range from CHF 20 to CHF 60, depending on the performance.
- Opening Hours:
  - Concerts typically start around 8 PM, but doors open at 7 PM for most events

- Description: Papiersaal is an eclectic music venue that hosts an impressive range of live performances, including rock, pop, electronic music, and indie acts. Located in a former industrial building, the venue has a cool, raw atmosphere that draws in music fans from across the city. Papiersaal's sound quality and intimate setting make it a top choice for catching live shows in Zurich.
- Website: Papiersaal Zurich

6. Kauft Die Musik (Kaufleuten Club)

- Location: Pelikanstrasse 18, 8001 Zurich
- Price: Tickets range from CHF 25 to CHF 80, depending on the event and artist.
- Opening Hours:
  - Monday to Saturday: 9 PM to late
  - Closed on Sundays
- Description: Kaufleuten Club is Zurich's iconic venue for both live music and clubbing. The club hosts a wide variety of performances, from live concerts by popular rock and pop bands to DJ sets and dance events. Known for its elegant interior and top-notch sound system, Kaufleuten is a perfect spot for enjoying an unforgettable night of live music and dancing.
- Website: Kaufleuten Zurich

7. Club Bellevue Zurich

- Location: Seefeldstrasse 1, 8008 Zurich
- Price: CHF 20 to CHF 60, depending on the artist and event.
- Opening Hours:
  - Open Friday and Saturday from 11 PM to late
- Description: For a night of electronic music and dancing, Club Bellevue is one of Zurich's best spots. Known for its pulsating beats and incredible light displays, this venue hosts some of the best international and local electronic DJs. It's a favorite among clubbers and those looking to enjoy Zurich's nightlife scene.
- Website: Club Bellevue Zurich

Summary

Zurich's vibrant cultural scene ensures that theatre, opera, and live music lovers have ample opportunities to enjoy world-class performances throughout the year. Whether you're attending a grand opera at the Zurich Opera House, experiencing contemporary theatre at Schauspielhaus Zürich, enjoying jazz at Moods Jazz Club, or dancing to electronic music at Kaufleuten, Zurich offers a diverse range of experiences that cater to all musical and theatrical tastes. Be sure to check performance schedules in advance to catch these cultural gems during your visit!

6.3 Traditional Swiss Cuisine and Where to Find It

Swiss cuisine reflects the country's diverse cultural influences, blending German, French, and Italian traditions to create a rich tapestry of flavors. Whether you're craving hearty mountain fare, delicate Swiss pastries, or world-famous cheeses and chocolates, Zurich is the perfect place to indulge in these culinary delights. Here's a guide to traditional Swiss dishes and the best places in Zurich to try them:

1. **Fondue**

- Description: Perhaps the most iconic Swiss dish, fondue is a rich and comforting meal made by melting a blend of Swiss cheeses (usually Gruyère and Emmental) with white wine, garlic, and a touch of kirsch (cherry schnapps). It's served with cubes of crusty bread for dipping. Fondue is often enjoyed in a social setting, making it a popular dish for groups.
- Where to Try It:
  - Swiss Chuchi Restaurant
    - Location: Rindermarkt 1, 8001 Zurich
    - Description: A cozy, traditional Swiss restaurant located in the heart of Zurich's Old Town. Famous for its fondue, Swiss Chuchi offers a variety of cheese fondues, as well as meat fondues and raclette.

- Price: CHF 30 - CHF 50 per person
- Website: Swiss Chuchi Restaurant
  - Le Dézaley
    - Location: Sihlstrasse 28, 8001 Zurich
    - Description: Known for its authentic cheese fondue, Le Dézaley is a traditional Swiss restaurant offering a rustic atmosphere and a menu full of Swiss classics. Their fondue is made with a blend of Gruyère and Vacherin cheeses.
    - Price: CHF 30 - CHF 50 per person
    - Website: Le Dézaley

2. Rösti

- Description: Rösti is a Swiss potato dish that is crispy on the outside and soft on the inside. It's often served as a side dish for breakfast or with a main course. While it originated in the German-speaking part of Switzerland, it is now loved across the country. Rösti is typically made with grated potatoes, butter, and salt, and sometimes includes ingredients like cheese, onions, or bacon.
- Where to Try It:
  - Kronenhalle
    - Location: Kreis 1, 8001 Zurich
    - Description: An upscale restaurant with a classic Zurich atmosphere, Kronenhalle offers a delicious Rösti made with carefully prepared ingredients. It's a favorite among locals and visitors alike.
    - Price: CHF 20 - CHF 35
    - Website: Kronenhalle
  - Hiltl
    - Location: Sihlstrasse 28, 8001 Zurich
    - Description: As one of the world's oldest vegetarian restaurants, Hiltl offers a range of Swiss and international dishes, including Rösti with various vegetarian toppings.
    - Price: CHF 15 - CHF 25
    - Website: Hiltl

3. Raclette

- Description: Raclette is a popular dish where melted cheese is scraped onto potatoes, pickles, and sometimes meats or vegetables. It is traditionally made with the Raclette cheese, which has a rich and creamy texture that melts beautifully. Raclette is often served in a social setting and is a perfect dish for groups.
- Where to Try It:
  - Restaurant Swiss Chuchi

- Location: Rindermarkt 1, 8001 Zurich
- Description: A must-visit place for traditional Swiss dishes, Swiss Chuchi also serves a classic raclette dish that is perfect for cheese lovers.
- Price: CHF 30 - CHF 45 per person
- Website: [Swiss Chuchi Restaurant](#)
    - Restaurant Sternen Grill
        - Location: Bellevueplatz, 8001 Zurich
        - Description: A casual restaurant that serves Raclette in a lively, outdoor setting, ideal for enjoying this dish with a glass of Swiss wine.
        - Price: CHF 25 - CHF 40
        - Website: [Sternen Grill](#)

4. Swiss Chocolate

- Description: Switzerland is world-famous for its chocolate, and Zurich is home to some of the best chocolatiers in the country. Swiss chocolate is known for its smooth texture and rich flavor, made from high-quality cocoa beans. Popular types include milk chocolate, dark chocolate, and white chocolate, often infused with unique flavors like hazelnuts, caramel, or fruit.
- Where to Try It:
    - Confiserie Lindt
        - Location: Bahnhofstrasse 69, 8001 Zurich
        - Description: The Lindt store in Zurich is the perfect place to indulge in premium Swiss chocolate. You can shop for a variety of chocolates or enjoy a delicious hot chocolate.
        - Price: CHF 5 - CHF 50 (depending on the product)
        - Website: [Lindt Chocolate](#)
    - Confiserie Bachmann
        - Location: Niederdorfstrasse 31, 8001 Zurich
        - Description: Known for its handmade chocolate truffles and pralines, Confiserie Bachmann offers a selection of exquisite Swiss chocolates made with high-quality ingredients.
        - Price: CHF 5 - CHF 35
        - Website: [Confiserie Bachmann](#)

5. Zürcher Geschnetzeltes

- Description: This traditional Zurich dish features sliced veal cooked in a creamy white wine sauce and served with Rösti. It's a rich, hearty dish that captures the essence of Zurich's comfort food.

- Where to Try It:
  - Restaurant Sternen Grill
    - Location: Bellevueplatz, 8001 Zurich
    - Description: Famous for its traditional Zurich-style dishes, Sternen Grill offers an authentic version of Zürcher Geschnetzeltes served with Rösti.
    - Price: CHF 30 - CHF 45
    - Website: [Sternen Grill](#)
  - Haus Hiltl
    - Location: Sihlstrasse 28, 8001 Zurich
    - Description: Known for offering both Swiss and vegetarian options, Hiltl serves a plant-based version of Zürcher Geschnetzeltes, using mushrooms and soy-based ingredients.
    - Price: CHF 25 - CHF 35
    - Website: [Hiltl](#)

Summary

Zurich offers a wealth of opportunities to enjoy traditional Swiss cuisine. Whether you're indulging in a rich fondue at Swiss Chuchi Restaurant, savoring a plate of creamy raclette at Le Dézaley, or tasting a chocolate treat from Lindt, the city's culinary scene is a must-explore for food lovers. With a wide range of restaurants and cafés offering both traditional and modern twists on Swiss classics, Zurich is sure to satisfy every palate. Make sure to try these delicious Swiss specialties to complete your cultural experience in Zurich!

Chapter 7. Outdoor Adventures

7.1 Parks and Gardens: Quiet Retreats in the City

Zurich may be a bustling urban center, but it is also home to several peaceful parks and gardens that provide a welcome respite from the city's fast pace. Whether you're looking for a spot to relax, enjoy a picnic, or take a peaceful stroll surrounded by nature, Zurich offers a variety of green spaces. Here's a guide to some of the best parks and gardens to explore in Zurich in 2025:

1. Zurich's Old Botanical Garden

- Location: Stadtgarten 5, 8001 Zurich
- Description: One of Zurich's oldest and most beautiful parks, the Old Botanical Garden is home to over 15,000 species of plants and trees. It's the perfect place to unwind in a serene environment with stunning views of the city and Lake Zurich. The garden also has several sculptures and quiet spots ideal for reading or meditation.
- Price: Free entry
- Opening Hours: Daily, 7:00 AM - 7:00 PM (summer), 7:00 AM - 5:00 PM (winter)
- Website: Old Botanical Garden

2. Chinese Garden

- Location: Seefeldquai, 8008 Zurich
- Description: The Chinese Garden is a tranquil space that offers a taste of Eastern serenity in the heart of Zurich. It was a gift from Zurich's sister city, Kunming, and features authentic Chinese architecture, a koi pond, and traditional plants. It's a peaceful retreat with a lovely lake view, perfect for a quiet afternoon.
- Price: Free entry
- Opening Hours: Daily, 9:00 AM - 7:00 PM (summer), 9:00 AM - 5:00 PM (winter)
- Website: [Chinese Garden Zurich](#)

3. Uetliberg Mountain and Surrounding Trails

- Location: Uetliberg, 8143 Zurich
- Description: Offering panoramic views of Zurich and the surrounding Alps, Uetliberg Mountain is a popular outdoor destination just outside the city. It features several hiking trails that wind through forests, offering a peaceful escape from the urban environment. Visitors can reach the summit by foot, bike, or a scenic train ride. The summit offers magnificent views of Zurich, and there's a restaurant at the top where you can relax and enjoy the scenery.
- Price: Free to access, CHF 20 - CHF 30 for the Uetliberg train ticket (round trip)
- Opening Hours: Open year-round, 24 hours (trains and facilities may vary seasonally)
- Website: [Uetliberg](#)

4. Zürichhorn Park

- Location: Seefeldstrasse, 8008 Zurich
- Description: Situated along the shores of Lake Zurich, Zürichhorn Park is an ideal spot for a peaceful walk or picnic. The park offers beautiful views of the lake, sculptures, and grassy areas for relaxation. It's also home to the Swiss National Museum and the Zurich Chinese Garden, which are worth a visit if you're in the area.
- Price: Free entry
- Opening Hours: Open daily, 24 hours
- Website: Zürichhorn Park

5. Zürich Wilderness Park

- Location: Zurich-West, 8004 Zurich
- Description: For those seeking more of a natural retreat, the Zürich Wilderness Park is a green oasis that offers trails through forests, wetlands, and meadows. It's an area dedicated to preserving Zurich's native wildlife and is perfect for those

wanting to immerse themselves in nature. It also offers educational opportunities with its interactive exhibits about the local flora and fauna.

- Price: Free entry
- Opening Hours: Daily, 8:00 AM - 7:00 PM
- Website: Zürich Wilderness Park

Summary

Zurich is home to a wealth of tranquil parks and gardens, providing the perfect balance between nature and city life. Whether you're exploring the historic Old Botanical Garden, enjoying the serenity of the Chinese Garden, or taking in the panoramic views from Uetliberg Mountain, these green spaces offer an ideal way to unwind and appreciate Zurich's natural beauty. From lakeside strolls to forest hikes, Zurich's outdoor spaces offer a peaceful retreat for every type of nature lover.

7.2 Hiking Trails Near Zurich

Zurich is surrounded by beautiful natural landscapes, offering a wide variety of hiking trails suitable for all levels of hikers. Whether you're looking for a leisurely walk with scenic views or a challenging mountain hike, Zurich's proximity to the Alps and other stunning natural areas provides endless possibilities for outdoor adventures. Here's a guide to some of the best hiking trails near Zurich in 2025:

1. Uetliberg Mountain Hike

- Location: Uetliberg, 8143 Zurich
- Description: The Uetliberg Mountain is one of Zurich's most popular hiking destinations, providing panoramic views of the city, Lake Zurich, and the Alps. The main hiking trail starts at the Triemli tram station and leads to the summit, a 2.5-hour walk offering incredible views along the way. For those seeking a shorter hike, the Planet Trail provides a gentle walk with scenic stops explaining the solar system.
- Difficulty: Easy to Moderate
- Duration: 2.5 hours (to the summit)
- Elevation Gain: 870 meters
- Price: Free entry
- Opening Hours: Year-round
- Website: Uetliberg

2. Felsenegg to Uetliberg

- Location: Felsenegg, 8702 Zurich
- Description: This stunning hiking route connects Felsenegg, a cliff on the opposite side of Lake Zurich, to Uetliberg Mountain. The trail offers breathtaking views of the lake and the surrounding mountains. Along the way, you'll pass through forested paths and open meadows, making it a peaceful yet invigorating journey.
- Difficulty: Moderate
- Duration: 3 hours
- Elevation Gain: 480 meters
- Price: Free entry
- Opening Hours: Year-round
- Website: Felsenegg

3. Sihlwald and Sihl River Hike

- Location: Sihlwald Nature Reserve, 8135 Zurich
- Description: Located just a short distance from the city center, the Sihlwald Nature Reserve offers a peaceful escape into a lush forest setting. This easy-to-moderate hike follows the Sihl River through the forest, providing a scenic route with the chance to observe local wildlife and flora. The nature reserve is ideal for a day of relaxation, picnicking, and birdwatching.
- Difficulty: Easy

- Duration: 2 hours
- Elevation Gain: 150 meters
- Price: Free entry
- Opening Hours: Year-round
- Website: Sihlwald

4. Greifensee Circuit

- Location: Greifensee, 8606 Zurich
- Description: For a peaceful lakeside hike, the Greifensee Circuit is an ideal choice. This 13-kilometer loop around Greifensee Lake offers picturesque views of the water and surrounding countryside, with opportunities for birdwatching and enjoying the local flora. The hike is mostly flat, making it an easy and enjoyable route for hikers of all abilities.
- Difficulty: Easy
- Duration: 3 hours
- Elevation Gain: 100 meters
- Price: Free entry
- Opening Hours: Year-round
- Website: Greifensee Circuit

Summary

Zurich is an ideal base for exploring the Swiss countryside and Alps, offering a range of hiking trails for every level. Whether you're interested in an easy lakeside stroll, a scenic mountain trek, or a nature-filled retreat in a local reserve, Zurich's hiking trails provide ample opportunities to enjoy the breathtaking beauty of the region. From the accessible Uetliberg Mountain to the challenging peaks of Pizol and Rigi, hiking enthusiasts can find plenty to explore just a short distance from the city.

7.3 Seasonal Highlights: Summer and Winter Activities

Zurich is a city that truly shines year-round, offering a diverse range of activities to match the changing seasons. Whether you're visiting during the warm summer months or the crisp winter season, there's always something to do in and around Zurich. Here's a look at the best seasonal activities for both summer and winter in Zurich:

Summer Activities in Zurich

1. Swimming and Water Sports at Lake Zurich

- Location: Lake Zurich, 8000 Zurich

- Description: Summer in Zurich means plenty of time spent by the lake. From swimming at the public beaches, such as Strandbad Mythenquai and Katzenbach, to engaging in water sports like paddleboarding, sailing, or rowing, Lake Zurich is the center of the city's summer leisure activities. Rent pedal boats, rowboats, or stand-up paddleboards from various vendors along the shore for a fun and active day on the water.
- Price: Free for swimming (some areas may charge CHF 5-10 for entry)
- Website: Strandbad Mythenquai

2. Outdoor Festivals and Events

- Location: Various locations in Zurich
- Description: Zurich is a hub for summer festivals, offering a mix of cultural celebrations, music festivals, food markets, and outdoor performances. Key events include the Zurich Street Parade (a massive electronic dance music festival) and the Zurich Openair (a music festival held in August). You can also experience traditional Swiss events like Sechseläuten, a spring festival in which a giant snowman effigy is burned to mark the start of summer.
- Price: Varies by event (some free, others require tickets)
- Website: Zurich Festivals

3. Hiking and Outdoor Exploration

- Location: Zurich's Surrounding Mountains and Countryside
- Description: Summer is the perfect time for hiking, and Zurich's surrounding mountains, such as Uetliberg and Felsenegg, offer easy access to scenic trails. From beginner-friendly routes to more challenging hikes, the region provides ample opportunities to explore Zurich's natural beauty. Consider taking a hike up Uetliberg Mountain for panoramic views of the city and the lake, or explore the Zurich Wilderness Park for a peaceful retreat in nature.
- Price: Free for hiking trails
- Website: Uetliberg Mountain Hikes

4. Boat Tours and Lake Cruises

- Location: Lake Zurich, 8000 Zurich
- Description: A boat tour is a must-do summer activity in Zurich. The Zürichsee-Schifffahrtsgesellschaft (ZSG) offers a variety of cruises, from short scenic tours to longer excursions that take you to nearby towns like Rapperswil. During the summer, the boats run frequently, allowing you to enjoy the stunning views of the lake, city, and surrounding mountains. Sunset cruises are especially popular for a romantic evening experience.

- Price: CHF 5-40 depending on the cruise duration
- Website: [ZSG Lake Zurich Cruises](#)

5. Open-Air Dining and Picnicking

- Location: Lake Zurich Promenade and Various Parks
- Description: Summer in Zurich is perfect for outdoor dining. Many restaurants along the lake, such as Seerose and Fischer's Fritz, offer outdoor seating with views of the water. You can also enjoy a picnic in one of Zurich's many parks, including the expansive Zurich Botanical Garden or the peaceful Enge Church Park. Grab some fresh Swiss cheese, bread, and wine, and enjoy a relaxing afternoon in the sunshine.
- Price: Varies by restaurant (CHF 30-60 per person for a meal)
- Website: [Fischer's Fritz](#)

Winter Activities in Zurich

1. Ice Skating on Lake Zurich

- Location: Lake Zurich, 8000 Zurich
- Description: As winter sets in, Lake Zurich freezes over, and the city's iconic Eisbahn (ice rink) pops up on the lake's surface. You can rent skates and glide over the frozen lake while enjoying views of Zurich's skyline and snow-capped mountains. If the lake isn't frozen, head to indoor ice rinks like the Dolder Ice Rink for some winter fun.
- Price: CHF 10-15 for rentals
- Opening Hours: Winter months, typically 9:00 AM - 7:00 PM
- Website: [Zurich Ice Rinks](#)

2. Christmas Markets and Holiday Celebrations

- Location: Zurich City Center and Various Locations
- Description: Zurich's Christmas markets are a festive delight, offering traditional Swiss holiday treats, handcrafted goods, and hot drinks. The Zurich Christmas Market at Bahnhofstrasse is the most famous, featuring over 150 stalls selling everything from Christmas ornaments to Swiss chocolates. The market at Werdmühleplatz is known for its beautiful Christmas tree adorned with Swarovski crystals.
- Price: Free entry, with purchases available starting at CHF 5
- Website: [Zurich Christmas Markets](#)

3. Skiing and Snowboarding in the Swiss Alps

- Location: Zurich (Day trips to ski resorts)
- Description: While Zurich itself doesn't have ski slopes, it's an ideal base for accessing some of the best ski resorts in Switzerland. Take a day trip to the nearby Engelberg or Flumserberg ski areas, where you can enjoy skiing, snowboarding, and snowshoeing in the breathtaking Swiss Alps. These resorts are easily accessible by train, making them perfect for a winter adventure.
- Price: Ski passes range from CHF 50-100 per day depending on the resort
- Website: Engelberg Ski Resort

4. Winter Hiking and Snowshoeing

- Location: Uetliberg, Flumserberg, and Surrounding Mountains
- Description: Zurich offers plenty of opportunities for winter hiking and snowshoeing. The Uetliberg Mountain transforms into a snowy wonderland in winter, with marked trails for both walking and snowshoeing. Similarly, the Flumserberg area provides snowshoe trails through peaceful winter forests, offering a tranquil winter escape from the city.
- Price: Free for hiking trails, rentals CHF 20-30 for snowshoes
- Website: Flumserberg Winter Hiking

Summary

Zurich offers a wealth of activities throughout the year, from the vibrant outdoor experiences of summer to the serene, snow-covered landscapes of winter. In the summer, enjoy swimming, water sports, and scenic cruises on Lake Zurich, while festivals, hiking, and outdoor dining add to the lively atmosphere. In winter, take advantage of the city's ice skating rinks, Christmas markets, and nearby ski resorts for a quintessential Swiss winter experience. Whether you're visiting in the warmer months or the colder season, Zurich promises to deliver unforgettable memories.

Chapter 8. Shopping in Zurich

8.1 Luxury Boutiques on Bahnhofstrasse

Bahnhofstrasse is Zurich's premier shopping street and one of the most famous in the world, offering a sophisticated mix of high-end luxury boutiques, flagship stores, and designer showrooms. This tree-lined avenue, which runs from Zurich's main train station (Zurich Hauptbahnhof) down to Lake Zurich, is the perfect destination for luxury shopping. Whether you're searching for iconic Swiss watches, fine jewelry, or the latest fashion from international designers, Bahnhofstrasse has it all.

Top Luxury Boutiques and Stores on Bahnhofstrasse

1. Chopard

- Location: Bahnhofstrasse 41, 8001 Zurich
- Description: Known for its fine Swiss craftsmanship, Chopard offers a stunning collection of luxury watches, jewelry, and accessories. The boutique is a haven for those seeking high-end timepieces with a timeless design.
- Price Range: CHF 2,000 - CHF 200,000+ (depending on the item)
- Opening Hours: Monday - Friday: 10:00 AM - 6:30 PM; Saturday: 10:00 AM - 5:00 PM
- Website: Chopard Zurich

2. Louis Vuitton

- Location: Bahnhofstrasse 75, 8001 Zurich
- Description: Louis Vuitton is synonymous with luxury, offering its signature monogrammed bags, luggage, and accessories. The boutique on Bahnhofstrasse provides a range of classic and seasonal collections for those who appreciate French elegance.
- Price Range: CHF 500 - CHF 5,000+
- Opening Hours: Monday - Friday: 10:00 AM - 7:00 PM; Saturday: 10:00 AM - 6:00 PM
- Website: [Louis Vuitton Zurich](#)

3. Gucci

- Location: Bahnhofstrasse 57, 8001 Zurich
- Description: Gucci offers a luxurious shopping experience with its high-end fashion collections, including ready-to-wear clothing, accessories, shoes, and iconic bags. The boutique's contemporary interior complements its eclectic and stylish product range.
- Price Range: CHF 300 - CHF 10,000+
- Opening Hours: Monday - Friday: 10:00 AM - 7:00 PM; Saturday: 10:00 AM - 6:00 PM
- Website: [Gucci Zurich](#)

4. Hermès

- Location: Bahnhofstrasse 62, 8001 Zurich
- Description: Hermès is a symbol of craftsmanship and luxury. Known for its leather goods, scarves, and famous Birkin bags, this boutique offers an unparalleled shopping experience for those looking for classic luxury items.
- Price Range: CHF 500 - CHF 25,000+
- Opening Hours: Monday - Friday: 10:00 AM - 7:00 PM; Saturday: 10:00 AM - 6:00 PM
- Website: [Hermès Zurich](#)

5. Rolex

- Location: Bahnhofstrasse 58, 8001 Zurich
- Description: As one of the most prestigious Swiss watch brands, Rolex offers a refined collection of timepieces at its boutique on Bahnhofstrasse. Known for their precision and elegance, Rolex watches are a symbol of status and style.
- Price Range: CHF 5,000 - CHF 50,000+

- Opening Hours: Monday - Friday: 10:00 AM - 6:30 PM; Saturday: 10:00 AM - 5:00 PM
- Website: Rolex Zurich

Summary

Bahnhofstrasse is Zurich's luxury shopping epicenter, offering a world-class selection of high-end boutiques from global brands such as Louis Vuitton, Rolex, Hermès, and Tiffany & Co. Whether you're looking for Swiss watches, designer handbags, or fine jewelry, Bahnhofstrasse provides a sophisticated and exclusive shopping experience. With its prime location and beautiful ambiance, it's a must-visit destination for any traveler seeking luxury and style in Zurich.

8.2 Local Markets and Artisan Finds

Zurich isn't just about luxury boutiques; it also boasts a variety of charming local markets and artisan shops where visitors can discover unique handmade goods, local crafts, fresh produce, and Swiss specialties. These markets provide an authentic and vibrant shopping experience, where you can take home a piece of Zurich's culture and craftsmanship. Here are some of the best markets and artisan finds in Zurich:

1. Zurich's Weekly Farmers' Markets

Location: Various locations throughout Zurich, including Bürkliplatz, Helvetiaplatz, and Stadelhofen

Price Range: CHF 5 - CHF 30 (depending on products)
Opening Hours:

- Bürkliplatz Market: Wednesdays and Saturdays, 6:30 AM - 11:00 AM
- Helvetiaplatz Market: Tuesdays, Fridays, and Saturdays, 8:00 AM - 12:00 PM
- Stadelhofen Market: Thursdays, 7:00 AM - 11:30 AM

Description:
Zurich's weekly farmers' markets are a great place to experience local flavors and products. The markets feature fresh, seasonal produce, artisanal cheeses, homemade breads, Swiss wines, and meats. Local farmers and producers sell their goods directly to customers, ensuring the highest quality and freshest items. It's a fantastic opportunity to purchase authentic Swiss ingredients, or simply enjoy the lively atmosphere while sampling local treats.

Website: Zurich Farmers' Markets

2. Zurich Christmas Markets

Location: Main market at the Werdmühleplatz, with smaller markets scattered around the city center
Price Range: CHF 5 - CHF 100+ (depending on items)
Opening Hours:

- Typically late November to December 24th, 11:00 AM - 9:00 PM daily
- Werdmühleplatz Christmas Market: 11:00 AM - 9:00 PM

Description:
Zurich's Christmas markets are a magical experience, especially during the holiday season. The markets feature a wide range of handcrafted ornaments, jewelry, Swiss Christmas decorations, knitted goods, and local handicrafts. You'll also find many stalls selling gourmet Swiss treats, such as hot chestnuts, mulled wine, and Swiss chocolate. These markets not only offer a chance to pick up artisan goods but also give visitors a cozy, festive atmosphere to enjoy.

Website: Zurich Christmas Markets

3. Stadelhofen's Flea Market

Location: Stadelhofen Train Station, Zurich
Price Range: CHF 1 - CHF 100+ (depending on items)
Opening Hours: Saturdays, 10:00 AM - 4:00 PM
Website: Stadelhofen Flea Market

Description:
The Stadelhofen Flea Market is a beloved local spot for treasure hunters and vintage lovers. Whether you're looking for antiques, second-hand clothing, collectibles, or quirky home decor, this market is the place to find unique items. Many of the vendors offer handmade products, vintage Swiss textiles, and locally crafted furniture. It's also a great place to find unique souvenirs that reflect Zurich's eclectic style.

4. Kunsthaus Zurich Artisans' Market (Kunsthaus Zürich)

Location: Kunsthaus Zurich (Zurich's Art Museum)
Price Range: CHF 10 - CHF 500+
Opening Hours: Held annually during special exhibitions or art fairs (check Kunsthaus Zurich website for event dates)
Website: Kunsthaus Zurich

Description:
Kunsthaus Zurich hosts artisan markets during various art exhibitions, bringing together a selection of local artisans who showcase their works. The market offers a range of handmade crafts, including jewelry, ceramics, paintings, and textiles. The products sold here are often inspired by Swiss art, culture, and design, making it a great place to find a meaningful and unique souvenir from Zurich.

5. Viadukt Market

Location: Viadukt (near the Wipkingen area)
Price Range: CHF 5 - CHF 50+ (depending on items)
Opening Hours: Monday - Saturday: 10:00 AM - 7:00 PM; Closed on Sundays
Website: Viadukt Market Zurich

Description:
The Viadukt Market is located under the iconic railway viaduct and offers a collection of artisan shops, craft stores, and local food vendors. The market is home to independent boutiques selling handmade leather goods, artisanal cheeses, local wines, and crafts. It's a popular spot for those looking for a mix of gourmet food, unique artisan creations, and an urban shopping atmosphere.

6. Zurich's Artisan Chocolate Shops

Location: Various locations throughout Zurich
Price Range: CHF 10 - CHF 100+
Opening Hours: Monday - Friday: 9:00 AM - 7:00 PM; Saturday: 9:00 AM - 6:00 PM (varies by store)
Description:

No trip to Zurich is complete without experiencing Swiss chocolate. Zurich is home to several artisan chocolate shops where you can taste and buy hand-crafted chocolates made by expert chocolatiers. Some of the most notable chocolatiers include Confiserie Bachmann, Lindt, and Teuscher. These stores offer a variety of premium chocolates, including truffles, pralines, and signature Swiss chocolate bars.

Website:

- [Confiserie Bachmann](#)
- [Lindt](#)
- [Teuscher](#)

Summary

Zurich offers a diverse range of local markets and artisan shops, perfect for visitors seeking authentic Swiss products, handmade goods, and local specialties. From the weekly farmers' markets offering fresh produce to the festive Christmas markets brimming with handcrafted decorations, there is something for everyone. Don't forget to explore the city's flea markets and artisan chocolate shops to bring home unique souvenirs and indulgent Swiss treats. These markets provide an opportunity to experience Zurich's rich cultural heritage while finding one-of-a-kind products that reflect the city's craftsmanship and creativity.

8.3 Swiss Watches, Chocolates, and Souvenirs

Zurich is a haven for those seeking iconic Swiss products, and the city's rich history in craftsmanship and design is showcased in its famous Swiss watches, high-quality chocolates, and a variety of charming souvenirs. Whether you're looking for a luxury timepiece, indulgent chocolate treats, or memorable keepsakes, Zurich offers a wide selection of authentic Swiss products that will make for perfect gifts or treasured mementos.

Swiss Watches: A Symbol of Precision and Craftsmanship

Switzerland is world-renowned for its watchmaking industry, and Zurich is home to a range of stores offering some of the finest timepieces in the world. When it comes to Swiss watches, Zurich's boutiques and watchmakers are the ultimate destination for watch enthusiasts and collectors.

1. Rolex

- Location: Bahnhofstrasse 58, 8001 Zurich
- Price Range: CHF 5,000 - CHF 50,000+
- Website: [Rolex Zurich]
- Description: Known for their timeless design and exceptional precision, Rolex watches are a symbol of luxury and craftsmanship. Rolex boutiques in Zurich offer a variety of models, including their iconic Oyster Perpetual and Datejust collections.

2. Patek Philippe

- Location: Bahnhofstrasse 53, 8001 Zurich
- Price Range: CHF 10,000 - CHF 100,000+
- Website: [Patek Philippe Zurich]
- Description: Considered one of the finest watchmakers in the world, Patek Philippe combines impeccable craftsmanship with innovative design. Their timepieces, such as the Calatrava and Nautilus, are highly coveted by collectors.

3. Omega

- Location: Bahnhofstrasse 38, 8001 Zurich
- Price Range: CHF 3,000 - CHF 10,000+
- Website: [Omega Zurich]
- Description: Omega is known for its sophisticated and versatile watches, such as the Seamaster and Speedmaster collections. A visit to Omega's Zurich store offers a chance to purchase a durable and stylish timepiece.

4. Swatch

- Location: Bahnhofstrasse 52, 8001 Zurich
- Price Range: CHF 50 - CHF 500+
- Website: Swatch Zurich
- Description: If you're looking for a more affordable and stylish Swiss watch, Swatch offers a fun and colorful range of watches, perfect for everyday wear. Swatch is known for its innovative designs and playful aesthetic.

Swiss Chocolates: Sweet Indulgence

Swiss chocolate is renowned worldwide for its quality and rich flavor. Zurich is home to some of the best chocolatiers, where you can indulge in handcrafted, artisanal chocolates or buy them as gifts for loved ones. Here are some must-visit chocolate stores in Zurich:

1. Lindt & Sprüngli

- Location: Bahnhofstrasse 10, 8001 Zurich
- Price Range: CHF 10 - CHF 50+
- Website: Lindt Zurich
- Description: Lindt & Sprüngli is one of the most famous Swiss chocolate brands, known for its smooth and luxurious chocolate. The Lindt store in Zurich offers a wide selection of pralines, truffles, and their famous Lindor chocolates, perfect for gifting or personal indulgence.

2. Teuscher

- Location: Bahnhofstrasse 31, 8001 Zurich
- Price Range: CHF 20 - CHF 100+
- Website: Teuscher Zurich
- Description: Teuscher is a luxury chocolate brand with an emphasis on quality ingredients and traditional Swiss techniques. Known for their exquisite Champagne Truffles, Teuscher's chocolates are handmade in Zurich, making them an authentic and indulgent souvenir.

3. Confiserie Bachmann

- Location: Located in various parts of Zurich, including Bahnhofstrasse and the airport
- Price Range: CHF 5 - CHF 50+
- Website: Bachmann Zurich
- Description: Confiserie Bachmann is a family-owned Swiss chocolatier that has been crafting high-quality chocolate and sweets for decades. Their chocolate bars, truffles, and other delicacies are made with the finest ingredients, offering a true taste of Switzerland.

Souvenirs and Swiss Specialties

In addition to watches and chocolates, Zurich offers a range of souvenirs that reflect the city's culture, heritage, and craftsmanship. These items make for memorable gifts or keepsakes to remind you of your time in Zurich.

1. Swiss Army Knives

- Location: Available at stores like Victorinox at Bahnhofstrasse 32, 8001 Zurich
- Price Range: CHF 30 - CHF 150+
- Website: Victorinox Zurich
- Description: A Swiss Army knife is a classic Swiss souvenir. Victorinox, the original creator of the Swiss Army knife, offers a wide selection of multi-tools, pocket knives, and other Swiss-made products.

2. Swiss Cheese

- Location: Available at local markets such as Zurich's weekly farmers' markets and stores like Chäsi Shop Zurich
- Price Range: CHF 5 - CHF 30+
- Description: Swiss cheese is a staple of Swiss culture, and Zurich is the perfect place to sample and purchase varieties like Gruyère, Emmental, and Raclette. These cheeses make excellent souvenirs for food lovers.

3. Swiss Cow Bells

- Location: Available at souvenir shops across Zurich, especially in the Old Town (Altstadt)
- Price Range: CHF 20 - CHF 100+
- Description: The iconic Swiss cow bell, traditionally used to call cows back to the barn, is a quirky and unique souvenir. Often beautifully decorated, it's a great way to bring a piece of Swiss culture home.

4. Swiss Textiles and Alpaca Wool

- Location: Shops like Swiss Made Shop (Bahnhofstrasse 28, 8001 Zurich) and Alpaka Shop Zurich
- Price Range: CHF 10 - CHF 150+
- Description: For a cozy and luxurious souvenir, consider purchasing Swiss-made textiles, such as Alpaca wool scarves, blankets, and knitted accessories. These items are made from high-quality, soft wool and are available in various patterns and colors.

Summary

Zurich is the perfect destination to shop for some of Switzerland's most iconic products, including world-renowned Swiss watches, luxurious chocolates, and traditional souvenirs. Whether you're looking for a fine timepiece from brands like Rolex and Patek Philippe, indulging in premium Swiss chocolate from Lindt or Teuscher, or picking up a unique Swiss souvenir like a Swiss Army knife or cowbell, Zurich offers a diverse range of options for every traveler. These authentic Swiss products not only make for exceptional gifts but are also a wonderful way to remember your visit to this charming and culturally rich city.

Chapter 9. Practical Information

9.1 Currency, Costs, and Tipping

Understanding Zurich's currency, general cost of living, and tipping culture is essential for having a smooth and enjoyable trip. This section provides a comprehensive guide to navigating Zurich's financial landscape, helping you make informed decisions during your visit.

Currency in Zurich

- Official Currency: Swiss Franc (CHF)
- Exchange Rate: 1 Swiss Franc (CHF) is generally equivalent to about 1 USD, but rates can fluctuate, so it's a good idea to check the latest exchange rates before you travel.
- Coins: CHF 0.05, CHF 0.10, CHF 0.20, CHF 0.50, CHF 1, CHF 2
- Banknotes: CHF 10, CHF 20, CHF 50, CHF 100, CHF 200, CHF 1000
- Currency Exchange: You can exchange foreign currency at banks, currency exchange offices, or ATMs throughout Zurich. It's best to use ATMs for a competitive exchange rate. Avoid exchanging currency at airports, as the rates can be less favorable.

Costs in Zurich

Zurich is known for being an expensive city, particularly when compared to other European destinations. However, there are plenty of ways to manage your budget. Here's an overview of common costs you'll encounter during your trip:

- Accommodation:

    - Budget: CHF 40 - CHF 100 per night (Hostels, budget hotels, guesthouses)
    - Mid-range: CHF 100 - CHF 250 per night (3-star hotels, private apartments)
    - Luxury: CHF 250 - CHF 500+ per night (5-star hotels, luxury resorts)
- Meals:

    - Budget: CHF 10 - CHF 20 for a simple meal at a casual restaurant or fast food
    - Mid-range: CHF 25 - CHF 50 for a three-course meal at a mid-range restaurant
    - Fine Dining: CHF 50 - CHF 100+ for a meal at high-end restaurants

- Transportation:

    - Single Tram/Bus Ticket: CHF 2.60 - CHF 4.80 (depending on distance)
    - Zurich Day Pass (unlimited travel): CHF 13 - CHF 25 (depending on zones)
    - Taxi: CHF 5 - CHF 10 base fare + CHF 3.50 - CHF 4 per km
- Attractions:

    - Museums: CHF 10 - CHF 20 for entry (Swiss National Museum, Kunsthaus Zurich)
    - Boat Trip on Lake Zurich: CHF 5 - CHF 20 for a one-hour cruise
    - Uetliberg Mountain: CHF 20 - CHF 40 for the train ride (round-trip)
- Shopping:

    - Souvenirs: CHF 5 - CHF 30 for items such as Swiss chocolates, keychains, and small souvenirs
    - Clothing: CHF 30 - CHF 100 for mid-range fashion brands (e.g., H&M, Zara)

Tipping in Zurich

Tipping is generally appreciated but not mandatory in Zurich, as service charges are often included in restaurant bills and prices are already higher. However, it is customary to leave a small tip for good service in certain situations.

- Restaurants   and   Cafés:

    - Service charge: Most restaurants include a service charge in the bill (around 10%).
    - Tip: It's customary to round up the bill or leave a small tip (CHF 1 - CHF 5) if the service was good. For higher-end restaurants, a tip of 5% to 10% is appreciated, but not expected.
- Taxis:

    - It's customary to round up the fare to the nearest franc or leave a tip of 5% to 10% for good service.
- Hotel   Staff:

    - Hotel staff generally don't expect tips, but if you have exceptional service from bellboys, concierge, or housekeeping, it's nice to leave CHF 1 - CHF 5 per service.
- Tour   Guides:

- For guided tours, it is appreciated to give a tip of CHF 5 - CHF 10 per person, depending on the length of the tour and the quality of the experience.
- Hotel Concierge: A tip of CHF 5 - CHF 10 is common if they assist with special requests, like booking tickets or organizing a special tour.

ATMs and Credit Cards

- ATMs: Widely available throughout Zurich, ATMs usually offer competitive exchange rates, and you can withdraw cash in Swiss Francs. Always check with your bank for any foreign transaction fees.

- Credit Cards: Most shops, restaurants, and services in Zurich accept major credit cards (Visa, MasterCard, American Express). However, it's always a good idea to carry some Swiss Francs in cash for small purchases or if visiting more rural areas.

- Contactless Payments: Switzerland is a cashless society in many areas, and contactless payments (via credit/debit cards or mobile wallets) are widely accepted.

Cashless and Digital Payments

Switzerland is one of the most advanced countries in terms of digital payments. Mobile payment apps like Apple Pay, Google Pay, and Twint are accepted at many locations across Zurich. Twint is particularly popular in Switzerland and allows users to make payments directly from their Swiss bank accounts via their smartphones.

Summary

Zurich is a relatively expensive destination, but with careful planning, you can enjoy the city within your budget. While many services already include service charges, it's customary to leave a small tip for excellent service in restaurants, taxis, and other service-based industries. The Swiss Franc (CHF) is the currency used, and cash can be withdrawn from ATMs or paid with credit/debit cards and mobile payment apps. Understanding the costs of accommodations, dining, transportation, and attractions will help you plan your spending more effectively, ensuring a stress-free trip to Zurich.

9.2 Language Basics and Communication Tips

Zurich is a multilingual city with German as the primary language. However, due to its international nature, English is widely spoken, especially in tourist areas. Understanding a few basic phrases and communication tips will make your trip even more enjoyable and ensure you connect better with locals.

Official Languages of Zurich

- German (Swiss German - Hochdeutsch): The primary language spoken in Zurich is Swiss German (Schweizerdeutsch), a dialect of German. It differs from standard German in terms of pronunciation, vocabulary, and grammar. However, the written language in Zurich is Standard German (Hochdeutsch).

- English: English is commonly spoken in Zurich, particularly in tourist areas, restaurants, hotels, and stores. Most people working in the service industry are fluent in English, and you will find English menus and signs in many places.

- Other Languages: Due to Zurich's international nature, you'll also hear languages like Italian, French, and Spanish being spoken, especially by the city's diverse expat population.

Basic German Phrases to Know

While English is widely spoken, learning a few basic German phrases can enhance your experience and show respect to the local culture. Here are some essential phrases to help you get by:

- Hello / Hi: *Hallo / Grüezi* (common greeting in Zurich)
- Goodbye: *Auf Wiedersehen / Tschüss*
- Please: *Bitte*
- Thank you: *Danke / Vielen Dank*
- Excuse me / Sorry: *Entschuldigung*
- Yes: *Ja*
- No: *Nein*
- How are you? *Wie geht's? / Wie geht es Ihnen?* (formal)
- I don't understand: *Ich verstehe nicht*
- Do you speak English? *Sprechen Sie Englisch?*
- How much does this cost? *Wie viel kostet das?*
- Where is...? *Wo ist...?*
- Restroom: *Toilette*

Common Swiss German Phrases in Zurich

- Grüezi mitenand! – "Hello, everyone!" (Common greeting in Zurich)
- Wie geht's? – "How are you?"
- Ich bin Tourist. – "I'm a tourist."
- Könnten Sie mir bitte helfen? – "Could you please help me?"
- Sprechen Sie Englisch? – "Do you speak English?"

- Haben Sie eine Speisekarte auf Englisch? – "Do you have a menu in English?"

Tips for Communicating in Zurich

1. English   is   Widely   Understood:

   - While Swiss German is the predominant language in Zurich, you'll find that many locals speak English, especially in central areas, hotels, and tourist destinations. Don't hesitate to ask if you're unsure of something, as most people will be happy to assist you in English.

2. Greet   with   a   Smile:

   - Swiss people value politeness, and a friendly greeting (such as "Grüezi") followed by a smile is a good way to start any interaction. It's customary to greet people with a handshake in more formal settings.

3. Use   Formal   Language   in   Public:

   - In Switzerland, formal language is often used when addressing strangers or people in a professional setting, especially older people. Use "Sie" (formal "you") when speaking to people you don't know or in business settings. "Du" (informal "you") is reserved for friends or people you're familiar with.

4. Be   Punctual:

   - Punctuality is highly valued in Zurich, and arriving late to an appointment or social gathering is generally seen as disrespectful. Try to arrive on time for activities, reservations, and public transport.

5. Politeness   and   Respect:

   - Swiss culture places importance on being respectful and polite in all forms of communication. When addressing others, use "Bitte" (please) and "Danke" (thank you) to show appreciation. It's also important to respect personal space and to avoid overly loud or animated conversations in public places.

6. Writing   a   Note   in   English:

   - If you need to write something (such as a note, order, or request) and you don't speak German, it's okay to write in English. Many people can understand it, and it's always appreciated if you make an effort to communicate in a local language.

Communication Tools and Apps

1. Google   Translate:

    ○ The Google Translate app is a handy tool for translating signs, menus, or phrases if you're unsure about something. It works offline as well, making it ideal for navigating unfamiliar situations.

2. Language   Learning   Apps:

    ○ If you want to prepare more extensively, apps like Duolingo or Babbel can help you learn basic Swiss German phrases before your trip, making your interactions smoother.

3. Public   Transportation   Apps:

    ○ Zurich has several apps to assist with navigating public transportation, such as the SBB Mobile app, which provides timetables and ticket purchasing options in multiple languages, including English.

Signs and Menus

- Signs in Zurich: Most public signage, including in restaurants, shops, and museums, will have information in both German and English, especially in tourist-friendly   areas.

- Menus: While many restaurants offer menus in English, especially in central Zurich, it's always good to ask if the menu is available in English. Some more traditional Swiss restaurants might only offer menus in German, but a basic understanding of the main ingredients can often be helpful.

Summary

Zurich is a multicultural city where English is widely spoken, but learning a few basic German phrases can make your experience even more enjoyable. Swiss German is the main language, but the formal nature of the language and polite greetings are important cultural elements. Most of the time, you will find it easy to communicate in Zurich, especially in tourist areas. The city's residents are friendly and generally open to helping visitors, so don't hesitate to ask for assistance. Using translation apps and knowing a few key phrases can ensure you feel comfortable and confident throughout your stay.

9.3 Visa and Entry Requirements

When traveling to Zurich, it's important to know the visa and entry requirements based on your nationality and the purpose of your visit. Switzerland is part of the Schengen Area, which means the visa policies are aligned with those of other Schengen countries. This section provides an overview of the general entry requirements for Switzerland and Zurich.

Visa Requirements for Zurich

Switzerland follows the Schengen visa policy, which means that a Schengen visa allows travelers to enter Zurich and other Swiss cities, as well as other countries in the Schengen Area, for short stays.

1. Schengen Visa (Short-Stay Visa)

- Purpose: For tourism, business trips, or visiting family/friends.
- Validity: The Schengen visa is typically valid for up to 90 days within a 180-day period.
- Visa Type: Type C (Schengen short-stay visa).
- Required Documents:
    o Valid passport (with at least 3 months' validity beyond your planned departure from the Schengen Area).
    o Completed visa application form.
    o Proof of travel insurance (coverage of at least €30,000 for medical emergencies).
    o Proof of sufficient funds for your stay (bank statements, employment letter, etc.).
    o Travel itinerary, including accommodation reservations or invitation letters if visiting friends/family.
    o Flight bookings (round trip).
    o A recent passport-sized photograph.
- Where to Apply: You can apply for a Schengen visa at the Swiss embassy or consulate in your home country. Some countries also allow applications through third-party visa centers like VFS Global.

2. Visa Exempt Countries (Schengen Area and Other Agreements)

- European Union (EU)/European Economic Area (EEA) Nationals:

- Citizens of the EU/EEA countries do not require a visa to enter Switzerland, including Zurich, for short stays (up to 90 days).
- Common EU countries: Germany, France, Spain, Italy, Netherlands, Sweden, etc.
- Other Visa-Exempt Countries:
  - Nationals from certain countries, including the United States, Canada, Australia, Japan, and several others, do not require a visa for short stays (up to 90 days) in Switzerland.
  - List of Visa-Exempt Countries:
    - United States, Canada, Australia, New Zealand, Japan, South Korea, Israel, and many others.
- If you are from one of these countries, you will simply need to show a valid passport upon entry to Switzerland.

Long-Term Stay and Residence Permits

If you plan to stay in Zurich for more than 90 days, you will need to apply for a long-term visa or residence permit. This is required for students, workers, or those planning to stay with family members.

Types of Long-Term Visas:

1. Student Visa: For individuals enrolled in a Swiss university or educational institution.
2. Work Visa: For those who have secured a job in Switzerland.
3. Family Reunification Visa: For individuals joining family members residing in Switzerland.
4. Entrepreneur or Self-Employed Visa: For individuals planning to start a business in Switzerland.

How to Apply:

- The application process for long-term visas generally requires:
  - Proof of enrollment (for students), job offer (for workers), or family relationship (for reunification).
  - Health insurance proof (mandatory for all Swiss visa types).
  - Financial proof showing that you can support yourself during your stay.

Applications should be made at the Swiss Embassy or Consulate in your home country or the country where you are a resident.

Customs and Border Control

Upon arriving in Zurich, you will need to pass through Swiss customs. Switzerland is part of the Schengen Area, so if you're traveling from another Schengen country, you may not have to go through customs. However, travelers from non-Schengen countries, such as the United States or the UK, will undergo immigration and passport control upon arrival.

- Passport Control: Ensure your passport is stamped upon entry and exit if you're not traveling within the Schengen Area.
- Customs Declarations: Switzerland has strict rules regarding the import of goods. If you are bringing in items worth over CHF 300 or more, you will need to declare them at customs.

Summary

Visa requirements for Zurich vary based on your nationality and the duration of your stay. Citizens from EU/EEA countries and many others are visa-exempt for short stays (up to 90 days). For longer stays, you will need to apply for a residence or long-term visa, depending on the purpose of your visit (e.g., work, study, family reunification). It is always advisable to check the latest entry requirements with the Swiss embassy or consulate in your home country before traveling, particularly regarding health regulations. Make sure to have all required documents in order to ensure a smooth entry into Zurich and Switzerland.

9.4 Safety and Health Tips for Travelers

Zurich is one of the safest cities in the world, with a low crime rate and high standards of healthcare. However, like any major city, it's important to take certain precautions to ensure your safety and well-being while exploring this vibrant Swiss destination. Here are some essential safety and health tips for travelers to Zurich:

General Safety Tips

1. Personal   Safety:

   - Low Crime Rate: Zurich is known for its safety, with crime levels significantly lower than in many other European cities. However, petty crimes such as pickpocketing can occasionally occur, especially in crowded areas like Bahnhofstrasse, tourist spots, and on public transportation.
   - Stay Aware of Your Belongings: Always keep your valuables, such as wallets, smartphones, and passports, close to you and avoid leaving them unattended, especially in busy tourist areas.
   - Nighttime Precautions: Zurich is generally safe at night, but it's always a good idea to stick to well-lit areas, especially in quieter neighborhoods. If

you're out late, consider taking a taxi or using ride-sharing apps like Uber to get back to your accommodation.

2. Emergency   Numbers:

   o Emergency Services: Dial 112 for emergency assistance (ambulance, police, fire).
   o Police: 117 (direct line to Zurich Police).
   o Ambulance: 144 (direct line for medical emergencies).

3. Road   Safety:

   o Pedestrian Safety: Zurich is a pedestrian-friendly city with many pedestrian crossings, but always pay attention to traffic signals and wait for the green light before crossing busy streets.
   o Cycling Safety: If you plan to rent a bike or cycle around the city, ensure you wear a helmet (though not required by law) and obey traffic rules. Zurich has well-marked cycling lanes throughout the city.
   o Public Transport Etiquette: Zurich's public transport system is efficient and safe. Avoid obstructing doorways when entering or exiting trams, buses, or trains. Keep your ticket handy, as ticket inspectors often board randomly.

Health Tips for Travelers

1. Health   Insurance:

   o It is highly recommended to have travel insurance that includes medical coverage for the duration of your stay in Zurich. Switzerland's healthcare system is excellent, but medical care can be expensive without insurance.
   o Check with your provider to ensure you are covered for any emergencies, and carry proof of your insurance with you at all times.

2. Health   Care   Facilities:

   o Zurich has a range of high-quality hospitals and clinics. In case of medical emergencies, you can visit the University Hospital Zurich (Universitätsspital Zürich), a major medical center with emergency services.
   o Pharmacies are plentiful across Zurich. If you need over-the-counter medications or advice on minor health issues, you can visit a pharmacy (apotheke). Some pharmacies have a 24-hour service for emergencies.

3. Water   Safety:

- Tap Water: Zurich's tap water is of exceptionally high quality and is safe to drink. In fact, Zurich is known for having some of the cleanest and freshest tap water in the world. You can refill your water bottle at public fountains throughout the city, many of which are supplied with fresh spring water.

4. Sun   Protection:

- Sunscreen: While Zurich has a moderate climate, you may still experience sunny days, especially in the summer months. Apply sunscreen to prevent sunburn, and wear a hat or sunglasses to protect yourself from UV rays.
- Hydration: Always carry a bottle of water and stay hydrated, particularly in the warmer months. It's important to avoid dehydration, especially if you're spending long hours outdoors exploring the city.

5. Altitude   and   Weather   Considerations:

- Zurich sits at an altitude of approx. 400 meters (1,312 feet) above sea level, which isn't high enough to cause altitude sickness. However, if you plan to visit mountainous areas such as Mount Uetliberg or the Swiss Alps, be mindful of higher altitudes and prepare accordingly.
- Winter Travel: If you're visiting during the winter months, be cautious of icy conditions on sidewalks and streets. Wear appropriate footwear with good grip, especially in the morning and evening when temperatures can drop below freezing.

6. Travel   Vaccinations:

- There are no specific vaccinations required for travelers coming to Switzerland, but it's always a good idea to be up to date on routine vaccinations (like tetanus, diphtheria, and measles).
- If you're traveling from a country with a risk of yellow fever, a yellow fever vaccination certificate may be required for entry.

Dealing with Jet Lag and Time Zone Adjustment

Zurich operates in the Central European Time (CET) zone, which is UTC+1 during the winter months and UTC+2 during the summer months (when daylight saving time is in effect).

1. Adjusting   to   Time   Zone   Differences:

- If you're coming from a time zone that's significantly different, you may experience jet lag. The best way to adjust is to gradually shift your sleeping schedule a few days before departure.

- Spend time outdoors in the natural light of Zurich to help reset your body clock.
2. Sleep   Tips:

- If you need to fight jet lag, try not to nap during the day and aim to sleep according to the local time as soon as possible.

Safety for Solo Travelers and Women

1. Solo   Travelers:

- Zurich is generally very safe for solo travelers, including solo women travelers. The city has a welcoming atmosphere, and people are usually willing to offer directions or assistance if needed.
- If you're a solo traveler, consider joining group tours or activities to meet fellow travelers and enjoy a more social experience.
2. Women   Travelers:

- Zurich is known for being safe and progressive, with a strong focus on gender equality and safety. Women can explore the city freely and confidently, even at night.
- However, as in any large city, it's always wise to stay vigilant and avoid poorly lit or deserted areas late at night.

Summary

Zurich is a safe, health-conscious city with excellent medical facilities, efficient public transport, and strict safety regulations. While Zurich is generally very safe for tourists, it's always wise to remain cautious of your belongings, especially in crowded areas. Ensure you have adequate travel insurance and are familiar with the city's emergency services and medical facilities. With these precautions, you can enjoy your trip with peace of mind, knowing that Zurich offers a secure and welcoming environment for all travelers.

Chapter 10. Appendices

10.1 Suggested Itineraries: One, Three, and Seven-Day Plans

Whether you're in Zurich for a short stop or an extended stay, there are plenty of exciting things to see and do. To help you make the most of your time, here are suggested itineraries for one, three, and seven days. Each plan includes top attractions, cultural experiences, and outdoor activities to match your pace and interests.

One-Day Zurich Itinerary: Highlights of the City

Morning:

- Old Town (Altstadt): Start your day by exploring Zurich's charming medieval old town. Visit Grossmünster Church and enjoy the scenic Limmatquai promenade along the river. Wander through the cobbled streets, stopping at local cafés for a traditional Swiss breakfast.

  - Time Needed: 2 hours
- Fraumünster Church: Don't miss the famous stained-glass windows designed by Marc Chagall. The church is one of Zurich's architectural gems.

  - Time Needed: 30 minutes

Late Morning:

- Bahnhofstrasse: Walk along one of the world's most exclusive shopping streets. Browse high-end boutiques, department stores, and luxury Swiss watch shops.
  - Time Needed: 1 hour

Afternoon:

- Lake Zurich: Take a leisurely walk along the lake or enjoy a boat cruise to experience Zurich from the water. The boat ride offers stunning views of the city and the Alps in the distance.

  - Time Needed: 1.5 hours
- Zurich's Art Scene: Visit the Kunsthaus Zurich (Zurich Art Museum) for an afternoon of world-class art. If you're interested in contemporary art, you might also check out the Zurich Museum of Design.

  - Time Needed: 1.5 hours

Evening:

- Zurich West District: Head to Zurich West for dinner at one of the trendy restaurants or bars in this revitalized industrial area. It's a great place to experience Zurich's modern cultural scene.
  - Time Needed: 2 hours

Three-Day Zurich Itinerary: A Deeper Dive into the City

Day 1: The Classic Zurich Experience

- Morning: Begin with a visit to Old Town and Grossmünster Church, followed by a stroll through Fraumünster and the surrounding squares. Take in the atmosphere at Bahnhofstrasse.
- Afternoon: Head to Lake Zurich for a relaxing boat cruise. Then visit the Zurich Art Museum or the Swiss National Museum.
- Evening: Enjoy dinner at Zurich West District, exploring its vibrant art galleries and culinary scene.

Day 2: Nature and Outdoor Adventure

- Morning: Take the Uetliberg Mountain train to hike or take in panoramic views of the city and the Swiss Alps.
  - Time Needed: 2-3 hours
- Afternoon: Explore Zurich Zoo, home to over 360 animal species. Alternatively, spend the afternoon cycling or walking along the Sihl River or visit one of Zurich's peaceful parks like Zurich Botanical Garden.
  - Time Needed: 2 hours
- Evening: Enjoy a traditional Swiss dinner at a restaurant in the city center or near the lake.

Day 3: Day Trips and Hidden Gems

- Morning: Take a day trip to Rhine Falls, Europe's largest waterfall, or head to Lucerne to explore its historic old town and the iconic Chapel Bridge.
- Afternoon: Continue exploring Lucerne or return to Zurich for a visit to the Zurich Museum of Design or a more intimate experience at the Swiss Craft Museum.
- Evening: End your trip with a relaxing evening at Kunsthaus Zurich or one of Zurich's famous restaurants, such as Zeughauskeller or Raclette Stube.

Seven-Day Zurich Itinerary: In-Depth Exploration and Day Trips

Day 1: Explore the City's Cultural and Historical Heart

- Morning: Visit Grossmünster and Fraumünster Churches, then wander through Old Town (Altstadt), making sure to stop at quaint cafés and bakeries.
- Afternoon: Take a leisurely walk down Bahnhofstrasse for shopping or window-shopping and visit the Zurich Art Museum for its world-class collections.
- Evening: Dine in Zurich West District, which offers great food options in a trendy, industrial setting.

Day 2: Dive Into Zurich's Nature

- Morning: Take a trip to Uetliberg Mountain for panoramic views or a scenic hike.
- Afternoon: Head to the Zurich Zoo or explore the Zurich Botanical Garden, perfect for nature lovers.
- Evening: Explore Zurich's lakeside area and take a sunset boat cruise on Lake Zurich.

Day 3: Explore the Surroundings

- Morning & Afternoon: Take a day trip to Rhine Falls, the largest waterfall in Europe, or spend the day in Lucerne, a picturesque lakeside city known for its medieval old town and Chapel Bridge.
- Evening: Return to Zurich for dinner in a local Swiss restaurant.

Day 4: Artistic Exploration

- Morning: Explore Kunsthaus Zurich and Zurich Museum of Design to experience Zurich's world-class art scene.
- Afternoon: Visit the Swiss National Museum to learn about the country's cultural history, or head to the Museum Rietberg to explore non-European art.
- Evening: Check out Zurich's local theater scene or catch a live music performance at a bar in the Zurich West District.

Day 5: Shopping, Gourmet, and Relaxation

- Morning: Spend the morning shopping in Zurich's high-end stores on Bahnhofstrasse and visit local artisan markets to pick up Swiss chocolates or handicrafts.
- Afternoon: Head to Lake Zurich for swimming or a boat trip, or visit the nearby Lindenhof Hill for a great view of the city.
- Evening: Indulge in a fine-dining experience at one of Zurich's Michelin-starred restaurants.

Day 6: Hiking and Adventure

- Morning: Head out on a hike to Jungfraujoch, one of the most famous mountain peaks in Switzerland, offering breathtaking views of the Alps.
- Afternoon: If you prefer something closer to Zurich, you can hike in the Sihlwald Forest or take a walk through the Zurich wilderness park.
- Evening: Wind down with a delicious dinner in the city or a casual fondue meal in the cozy Raclette Stube.

Day 7: Relax and Discover Hidden Gems

- Morning: Take a slow morning stroll around Zurich's lesser-known neighborhoods, like Kreis 3 or Kreis 4, where you can find unique cafes, hidden courtyards, and cool street art.
- Afternoon: Visit the Kunsthalle Zurich or the Felsenegg Cable Car for stunning views of the city.
- Evening: Finish your journey with a quiet evening at Zurich Opera House or a scenic dinner on the banks of Lake Zurich.

Summary

Whether you're in Zurich for just one day or planning a week-long getaway, there are countless ways to explore this beautiful Swiss city. The one-day itinerary focuses on key highlights, while the three-day plan offers a deeper dive into the city and nature. For those with more time, the seven-day itinerary includes a mix of city exploration, outdoor adventures, and day trips to nearby destinations like Rhine Falls, Lucerne, and Jungfraujoch. This range of itineraries ensures you experience the best of Zurich at your own pace.

10.2 Useful Apps and Websites for Travelers

When visiting Zurich, having the right tools at your fingertips can make your trip smoother and more enjoyable. Here's a list of essential apps and websites that can help you navigate the city, discover attractions, and enhance your overall experience.

1. Zurich Tourism Official Website

- Website: www.zuerich.com
- Description: The official tourism website for Zurich is a must-visit resource for all travelers. It provides up-to-date information on attractions, events, activities, and practical details like transportation and accommodations.
- Features:
  - Detailed event calendars
  - City guides and itineraries
  - Interactive maps
  - Offers and discounts for tourists

2. SBB Mobile

- App (iOS/Android): SBB Mobile (Swiss Federal Railways)
- Website: www.sbb.ch

- Description: This app is essential for planning train journeys in Switzerland, including routes, schedules, and ticket purchases. It also integrates local public transportation information, such as trams and buses.
- Features:
    - Real-time train and tram schedules
    - Route planning with multiple transport options
    - Mobile ticket purchase
    - Notifications for delays or cancellations

3. ZVV – Zurich Public Transport

- App (iOS/Android): ZVV (Zurich Transport Network)
- Website: www.zvv.ch
- Description: ZVV covers all the local public transport in Zurich, including buses, trams, and trains within the city and surrounding areas. The app allows you to buy tickets, plan your journey, and check timetables.
- Features:
    - Detailed transport schedules
    - Ticket purchasing options
    - Route planning for easy navigation within Zurich

4. Google Maps

- App (iOS/Android): Google Maps
- Website: maps.google.com
- Description: Google Maps is one of the best navigation tools to explore Zurich. You can use it to find the fastest routes for walking, biking, driving, or using public transport. It also offers information on local businesses, attractions, and user reviews.
- Features:
    - Turn-by-turn navigation
    - Offline maps
    - Recommendations for local restaurants, attractions, and stores
    - Traffic conditions and alternative routes

5. Citymapper

- App (iOS/Android): Citymapper
- Website: www.citymapper.com
- Description: Citymapper is an excellent app for navigating Zurich's public transport system. It integrates real-time data for trains, trams, buses, and walking routes, providing you with the fastest and most efficient ways to get around.

- Features:
  - Real-time public transport data
  - Detailed step-by-step route guidance
  - Alerts for any disruptions in your route

6. TripAdvisor

- App (iOS/Android): TripAdvisor
- Website: www.tripadvisor.com
- Description: TripAdvisor is a great app for finding recommendations on things to do in Zurich. With thousands of reviews from other travelers, you can explore local attractions, restaurants, and hotels to make informed decisions about where to go and what to see.
- Features:
  - User reviews and ratings
  - Popular tourist attractions
  - Restaurant, hotel, and activity recommendations
  - Travel forums for Q&A with fellow travelers

7. Uber

- App (iOS/Android): Uber
- Website: www.uber.com
- Description: Uber operates in Zurich, making it a convenient app for quick transportation across the city. Whether you need a ride to the airport, a restaurant, or a museum, Uber is a reliable alternative to taxis.
- Features:
  - Quick ride bookings
  - Fare estimator
  - Options for different types of rides (UberX, UberBLACK, etc.)

8. TheFork

- App (iOS/Android): TheFork
- Website: www.thefork.com
- Description: TheFork helps you discover the best dining experiences in Zurich. You can browse through restaurants, make reservations, and often get exclusive deals.
- Features:
  - Restaurant reservations with discounts
  - User reviews and ratings
  - Food photos and menus

9. Yelp

- App (iOS/Android): Yelp
- Website: www.yelp.com
- Description: Yelp is a great app for finding local restaurants, shops, and activities in Zurich. It includes user reviews, photos, and ratings, helping you make decisions on where to eat, shop, or explore.
- Features:
  - Local restaurant and shop recommendations
  - Reviews and photos from locals and tourists
  - Opening hours, addresses, and contact information

10. Swiss Travel Pass Mobile App

- App (iOS/Android): Swiss Travel Pass
- Website: www.swiss-travel-pass.com
- Description: This app is designed for visitors holding a Swiss Travel Pass. It gives you access to free travel on public transportation and discounts on various attractions, museums, and tours across Switzerland.
- Features:
  - Real-time travel information for Swiss public transport
  - Discounts for over 500 attractions
  - Digital Swiss Travel Pass storage

11. XE Currency

- App (iOS/Android): XE Currency
- Website: www.xe.com
- Description: XE Currency is the go-to app for currency conversion. It provides real-time exchange rates for Swiss Francs (CHF) and other global currencies, ensuring you're always up to date on the best exchange rates.
- Features:
  - Real-time exchange rate data
  - Currency conversion calculator
  - Offline mode for quick conversions on the go

10.3 Emergency Contacts and Numbers

When traveling to Zurich, it's essential to be prepared for any emergencies. Here is a list of important emergency contacts and services to ensure your safety and well-being during your trip.

1. General Emergency Number

- Phone: 112
- Description: This is the European emergency number, which connects you to police, fire, or medical services across Switzerland. It works for all types of emergencies and is available 24/7.

2. Police

- Phone: 117
- Address: Kantonspolizei Zürich, Polizeipost Werdstrasse 69, 8004 Zürich, Switzerland
- Website: www.polizei.ch
- Description: For non-emergency police inquiries, call the local Zurich police. They are available for situations like theft, lost items, or public disturbances. For immediate emergencies requiring police presence, call 117.

3. Fire Department

- Phone: 118
- Address: Feuerwehr Zürich, Feuerwehrstrasse 1, 8045 Zürich, Switzerland
- Website: www.feuerwehr.ch
- Description: In case of fire, accidents, or hazardous materials, the fire department can assist with emergency responses. Dial 118 for urgent situations requiring fire services.

4. Ambulance and Medical Assistance

- Phone: 144
- Description: If you need immediate medical attention, call 144. This number connects you directly to the ambulance service for emergencies, including accidents, medical conditions, or other urgent health-related issues.

5. Zurich Poison Control

- Phone: 145
- Description: For poisoning emergencies, such as ingestion of harmful substances or exposure to dangerous chemicals, call the poison control center at 145. They provide immediate medical advice and assistance.

6. Zurich Hospitals and Medical Centers

- University   Hospital   Zurich   (Universitätsspital   Zürich)
    - Phone: +41 44 255 11 11
    - Address: Rämistrasse 100, 8091 Zürich, Switzerland
    - Website: www.usz.ch
    - Description: One of Zurich's leading hospitals, providing a wide range of medical services including emergency care, surgery, and specialized treatment.
- Hospital   Triemli   (Spital   Triemli)
    - Phone: +41 44 416 11 11
    - Address: Birmensdorferstrasse 497, 8063 Zürich, Switzerland
    - Website: www.spital-triemli.ch
    - Description: Another major hospital in Zurich with comprehensive medical services, including emergency and urgent care.

7. Zurich Tourist Information

- Phone: +41 44 215 40 00
- Address: Zürich Tourism, Bahnhofstrasse 4, 8001 Zürich, Switzerland
- Website: www.zuerich.com
- Description: If you need help with general information or if you're lost or facing difficulties while navigating Zurich, you can contact the official Zurich Tourist Information Center.

8. Zurich City Ambulance

- Phone: +41 44 221 44 44
- Description: If you are seeking immediate medical transport services in Zurich, call this number to arrange for city ambulance assistance.

9. Embassy Contacts (For U.S. Citizens)

- U.S. Embassy in Switzerland
    - Phone: +41 44 285 18 18
    - Address: U.S. Embassy, Embassy Way 1, 3003 Bern, Switzerland
    - Website: ch.usembassy.gov
    - Description: The U.S. embassy provides consular assistance for American citizens in need of help, including lost passports, legal issues, or emergencies abroad.

10. Swiss Travel Hotline

- Phone: +41 900 300 300
- Description: For general travel inquiries, including information about trains, transportation schedules, and travel assistance within Switzerland, you can contact this hotline.

11. Zurich Taxi Service (For Emergency Transport)

- Phone: +41 44 444 44 44
- Description: This is the main taxi service number in Zurich. Taxis are available 24/7 and can be a reliable option for emergency transport, especially if you're in need of a ride to a hospital or other urgent location.

Summary

Having the right emergency contacts at hand is crucial for a safe and stress-free visit to Zurich. Whether you're facing a medical emergency, getting lost, or needing assistance with other unexpected situations, the above contacts will provide you with the necessary support. Always ensure you have access to these important numbers before you travel.

Printed in Dunstable, United Kingdom

71699953R00074